Restored

a story of

Finding Hope

and

Redefining Intimacy

by

Paul C. Talley Sr. and Suzanne Talley

Restored: Finding Hope and Redefining Intimacy

Copyright © 2016 by Paul C. Talley Sr. and Suzanne Talley

Published in the United States by CreateSpace and Paul C. Talley Sr. and Suzanne Talley.

Scripture references are from the following sources:

The King James Version

The New American Standard Version

Editorial Team: Lisa Gravitt, Jason Holmes, Eric Dennison

Cover by Designed by Mandii Erwin

Photo by Mandii Erwin

Printed in the United States

Library of Congress Cataloging in Publication Data

ISBN-13: 978-1523976454

ISBN-10: 1523976454

Dedication

This book is dedicated to each Couple who is fighting for their marriage as they read this book, to every Pastor needing more resources, and to you who was given this book to read by a friend or family member... we hope it is all and even more then you expected!

Table of Contents

Part Three: Restoration of Ministry to Broken Hearts by Paul and Suzanne Talley
105-188

Acknowledgements

We first want to give all the glory to God the Father and our Lord Jesus Christ for *"we know that God causes all things to work together for good to those who love God, to those who are called according to His purpose"* - Romans 8:28. His patience with us has been unbelievable. His love to us has been indescribable. His grace to us has been unstoppable. His forgiveness has been uncontainable. His mercy to us has been continual.

We also want to thank our children PJ, Benjamin, Caleb and Elizabeth for enduring this journey with us. You were wounded in different ways through our unhealthy relationship in the first 18 years of marriage and the years of recovery from it. We are deeply sorrowful for that but we hope you have been able to learn through our experience of repentance and forgiveness. We hope and pray that our journey has been and will be a guide to you throughout your single and married lives. We love you all and hope you always know that we will be there for you in the struggles that your journeys will bring.

We as well would like to express our gratitude to the people and leadership of *Shades Mountain Independent Church* in Hoover, Alabama. Your acceptance, love and forgiveness have been a model to us both. A special thanks to the former pastor, Harry F. Walls III, for your wisdom, kindness and special care through those hard days. You stood by us and believed in us in ways that no one else has and we are eternally thankful. Without this church and their leadership's guidance through our restoration process this book would not have been possible. Your loving application to us of church discipline and restoration should be a model to all churches.

We cannot express in words the gratitude that we have for Eli Machen. Your wisdom, care and patience as you guided our stubborn wills through this recovery process have been unrivaled. Your humble instruction, through our false spirituality, has been instrumental in our formation as children of God. There is no way to know where your instruction and the truths that we present in this book begin and end as they are interwoven throughout. You have been our Apostle Paul! We are your students and we have tried to be true and to be faithful to entrust the truths you have taught us to others. We have tried to live by the principles found in II Timothy 2:2 (KJV); *"And the things that thou hast heard of me among many witnesses, the same commit thou to faithful men, who shall be able to teach others also."*

This book is one way we are trying to entrust them to others. Your true reward will be found in heaven when you stand before our God and He will say; *"Well done, thou good and faithful servant: thou hast been faithful over a few things, I will make thee ruler over many things: enter thou into the joy of thy Lord"*. Matthew 25:21 (KJV). We are convinced that you will be a "ruler over many things" in the kingdom to come because of your faithfulness.

Last but not least, a special thanks to Patrick Carnes, his staff (especially Tami VerHelst), and the entire IITAP (The International Institute for Trauma and Addiction Professionals) faculty for their powerful training imparted to Paul as a PSAP. Patrick Carnes profound understanding of sexual addiction, recovery, and his development of the *Pastoral Sexual Addiction Professional* (PSAP) program has been instrumental in the saving of thousands from the stronghold of sexual addiction. It was an honor to sit at his and the other faculty members feet and absorb the vast knowledge they gave in this training. Paul considers it an honor to be called a PSAP.

Introduction

We count it an honor that you have chosen to read our book. Our desire is to encourage you on your journey of recovery or to help you begin this journey that Christ is calling you to carry out. We pray that you will **Find Hope** and start the process of **Redefining Intimacy** as you read.

We like the simple definition of intimacy that Dannah Gresh gives in her book, when defining the Hebrew word *yada* that is used for sexual intimacy in the Old Testament. Dannah says yada can be defined as "to know, to be known, and to be deeply respected" (What Are You Waiting For? The One Thing No One Ever Tells You About Sex 2011, Waterbrook Press). We have adopted that as our general definition for intimacy (sexual and non-sexual)

We want you to find the freedom to know your spouse, to be known by your spouse and for you both to have a deeply mutual-respectful relationship. We can say that God has done and continues to do that miraculous change in our marriage and we pray that He will do the same for you... there is Hope and we pray you find it in these pages!

In the following pages you will read our story from three points of view. Part One, **Restoration of a**

Betrayed Heart, is Suzanne's story and her focus is on her journey from simple prayers for change to seeing how God chose to answer those prayers. Her story starts with a simple prayer crying out to God and ends with her being the answer to many cries for help. She allows you to see her broken heart, the profoundness of her pain, how she got to the point that she needed recovery for herself, and her desire to help others. Suzanne's transparency should be a great encouragement to anyone whose heart has been betrayed. Her desire is to give you hope as she has found.

Part Two, *Restoration of a Dark Heart*, is Paul's story and goes deeper into his pain building up to the road to restoration. It gives you a look into the heart of a young boy/man who on the outside looks as if all is "ok" but on the inside the pain and wounds he carries are dark and very destructive. He describes what he ran to in a very open and frank way. Paul's transparency is a call to everyone to bring *things into the light and no longer be controlled by the darkness*. His honesty of his pain that God turned into inward peace and freedom should give us all hope to live in the light.

Part Three, *Restoration of ministry to Broken Hearts*, is our story, which shows the conclusion of God working all things out for our good and His glory. It shows how God clearly answered Suzanne's prayers by birthing a powerful ministry of reconciliation and restoration of marriages in crisis. It shares the vision of

Christian Marriages In Crisis (CMIC) and how Paul and Suzanne see God expanding this ministry in the future.

PART ONE

Restoration of a Betrayed Heart

by Suzanne F. Talley

Introduction

I will be taking you on my journey of recovery but I also want to give you some of the tools that saved my marriage. I hope to encourage you to start your own journey. I know it is very scary, but it is worth it. If you are struggling in your marriage, you need to know there is *HOPE*.

This book is not about my husband's "moral failure" but about our journey of healing and how God has taken a MESS and made it a MESSage. How He took a TEST and made it a TESTimony. I will be focusing on my own need for healing that came about through several prayers that I prayed and how God answered my prayers in unexpected ways. I have heard all my life, "Be careful for what you ask for." Well, this has been one of those moments for sure. I didn't ask for the chaos that occurred in my life, but I did ask for God to change me. Through the chaos, God did change me, and He will continue to change me until the day I meet Him face to face.

My prayer is that you will hear my testimony and be willing to take the challenge to relinquish control over your own life as I did and allow God to purify you and mold you into the person He wants you to be.

Chapter ONE

Prayers for Change

God Spiritually Preparing Me for a New Journey

It was May of 2004; I sat in the room with a group of women and held back my tears as we studied God's Word together. I didn't know then what the future held for me, but I knew that I was ready for God to do incredible things in my life. I don't think that I ever felt so close to the Lord before in all my life. I was highly involved in my church. I sang in the choir, I helped with the children's choir. I was on the Women's Retreat committee, helped start a Hispanic ministry, and was asked to join the women's ministry team. I started writing in a journal a few months before and the following are some of my entries.

Sept. 15th 2003
I haven't written in a while. This study is going to be powerful! I know that I'm headed for a <u>hard</u> time! I pray for the strongholds that Satan has on my life to be lifted and that the Power of the Holy Spirit will overcome those strongholds in my life. Help me Lord!!

May I take 1 Peter 5:6-9 to heart, and remember that I need to be on the alert and self-controlled because my enemy is on the prowl. I can stand firm knowing that my sisters in the faith are going through the same sufferings.

Paul is in Romania. "Lord, I pray for God to be in complete control over him! God grant him wisdom and strength. Give him rest as he sleeps and vibrancy as he is awake. I pray that much be accomplished and for hearts to be healed."

October 29th 2003
Wow, how the Lord is working on me! I can't believe where He's taking me. The Bible Studies that I've been in have been such a blessing. I'm amazed at what God will do when you just ask. In both Bible studies, I've basically been learning the same thing and that is that God has made me righteous! I'm not an unlovely Creature. I am a child of the King and I am special because of what He has made me to be. I owe Him all the praise and honor for everything. I give thanks to God for all that He's done and for all that He's going to do. Praise His Name! If God sent His own son to take my place on the cross, then I can certainly trust that He has proven His love for me. Because of the Blood of Jesus, I am redeemed. The old nature died with Christ and the new ownership has made me alive! Therefore I do not have to live in defeat. I have Victory over sin. God is on my side. Who can stand a chance against me?!

Through these bible studies I began to pray for change. One of those prayers specifically that I prayed was, "God, remove the scales from my eyes to see the things that need to be changed in me."

Expand Our Boarders

Paul and I had been Missionaries for eighteen years. We lived in Costa Rica for one year, Honduras for nine years and then in Alabama as Latin American Director for our mission for eight years. We shepherded eighteen families in several countries: Honduras, El Salvador, Peru, Albania, and Romania. The families that were in Albania and Romania were from El Salvador and Guatemala and had now become Missionaries to another country. Paul would often travel to each of those countries to care for those families. He would travel about once every six weeks for a week or two at a time.

In April of 2004, Paul and I went to Peru for a church conference. I don't remember too much about the conference. It was to dedicate a new building for ministry that Paul oversaw in Peru. Paul and I both ministered there; he spoke and I sang. The director of our mission also spoke one evening. He spoke on the *Prayer of Jabez*. It was before the Bruce Wilkinson book based on 1 Chronicles 4:10 became so wide-spread, and I had never heard anyone preach that message before. I remember praying a prayer that God would *expand our borders and bless us indeed.*

After that conference, the others returned back to the states while Paul and I used the rest of the trip to be with one of the missionary couples, whose marriage was in trouble. The wife had been unfaithful to her husband and he wanted to forgive her and stay in the marriage, but she was struggling with being with him. It was a tough trip for both of us. I normally didn't travel with Paul, but we had wanted to start traveling together and we felt God moving in us to work more as a team with couples that were hurting.

Paul had great insight and I sat in amazement at how he could see things that weren't so obvious. We worked great together. It seemed as though when we left Peru, God was going to heal their marriage and that He had chosen us to be instruments of his Power and Grace. My prayers seemed to begin to be answered and I thought that this was God *expanding our borders*.

We had planned on continuing to work with this couple and expected great things. Little did we know our enemy had planned something huge to keep this from happening, and so he took his shot at us. This is one of the next entries that I wrote:

June 1, 2004
Well, our lives have changed in a way I never thought would be possible. I feel like my life has all been a lie. What we thought was a great marriage now seems so

challenged. But God in his faithfulness has answered a prayer that I prayed at the beginning of this journal. I am truly broken. Paul is truly broken and God has our complete attention. In so many ways, I feel as though we get a new start. But it is going to be a scary journey.

It all started on May 11th. Paul took a trip to Albania and while on a layover in Amsterdam he was brutally attacked by Satan's army and he lost the battle. He didn't even see it coming. He immediately got his ticket changed and came running home a broken man devastated at his failure and the pain he now had brought upon me and his family. He was devastated at the loss of his ministry of eighteen years.

I came home that day to find out that Paul had not ever made it to his destination. As I walked through the door, he was in our basement waiting for me. He had a look of terror on his face. I thought someone had died. Who would it have been? How in the world would he have known before me? I was confused. I said, "What's going on? What's wrong?" He said, "Please sit down, I have to tell you something." Paul was struggling to get the words out, and I felt so badly for him to be the one to give me this horrible news. Then those words I never in my life thought I would hear coming from my husband: "I have been unfaithful to you". Those words left me shocked and devastated. How? What? Where?

I thought that I was having one of my terrible nightmares that I had had so many times during our marriage. I just wanted to wake up, hit Paul as I had done so many times before, and then he'd laugh at me and say, "I would never do that to you, honey." I began hitting myself so that I would wake up. He grabbed my hands because I was making marks on my face from hitting myself so hard. I fell to the ground in a fetal position. I had wished someone would have really have died. I could have made sense of that. But this? How could this make sense?

After the initial shock, I ended up angrily demanding to have someone come over. Our pastor, our mission agency director….someone to, "HELP ME!!!" I needed someone to make sense of this. This isn't my life! This is what happens to couples in conflict; couples who had a bad marriage. NOT MY MARRIAGE! I demanded, "If we are going to get through this, we have to have counseling, finally!" I shouted, "NOW ARE YOU GOING TO LISTEN TO ME?". You see, Paul and I did have conflict throughout our marriage but I would always become 'submissive' again and things would then be ok… at least until the next fight.

Chapter TWO

The Journey Begins

God Stripping Away the Idols

We took a pretty hard hit and it seemed to be completely devastating, but I can now see it as God answering my prayers. I had prayed for Him to purify my heart, and to purify my home. I had prayed for Him to remove the scales off my eyes and to see the truth. When He did, it wasn't too pretty.

Although Paul had been bombarded and was truly attacked by Satan, there were many things that we began to discover that led him to that dreadful day. I also began learning the things that made me do what I do and why I often find myself in bondage.

Just like experiencing a death in the family, you have to grieve when facing a trauma like this. There are many stages of grief, and I experienced them all. Sometimes you can stay in one stage longer than others and almost always there are stages that are repeated before true healing can occur.

When you encounter any type of trauma you are going to experience these stages of grief to some extent. Because of the trauma, I needed time to get away and start healing; I ended up going to a nice hotel in town to get away. I felt like everyone would worry about me if I went alone, so I asked my mom to go with me.

It was good to get away. I was able to cry and even laugh with my mom. We had to go shopping because I had kind of lost my mind while packing for our little adventure. While all of this is funny now, it sure wasn't then. I couldn't think straight to pack my bag if my life had depended on it! I had Pajama bottoms and no Pajama top. I had no underwear, but I had about 3 bras. I had no matching outfits at all. So, since I had no clothes we had to go shopping. I love to shop so that was a kind of therapy for me.

That night at the restaurant, we had a very strange waiter. He said, "We have room service, you know, so if you get a hankerin' for a termater just give us a call." So, for a long time after that we would call each other up and ask, "Hey, do you have a hankerin' for a termater?"

I think I may have cycled through every stages of grief during those couple of days at the hotel. Having my mom there was still a distraction for me to not face my pain (shock and denial stage of grief). So, I asked her to go on home and I was going to stay another night. I really just needed to be alone. I had no car, but I didn't plan on going anywhere anyway. I told her that if I felt like eating or drinking I would just order room service. I would call someone to come get me when I was ready to leave.

I had not slept the whole night before, so after Mom left to go home, I finally was able to cry out before God and get all the emotions out (Anger and Bargaining stages of grief) and then I fell asleep (Depression stage of grief). As soon as I woke up, I felt Jesus whisper, "Call Paul and ask him to take you to go see *The Passion*" which was in the theaters at that time. I knew that the visions that were in my head needed to be replaced by a new vision. I would never be able to forgive him as long as that is what I was seeing.

So, I called Paul and said, "Hey, do you want to take me to see a movie?" (Testing stage of grief) Of course this totally floored him. I can only imagine that he thought I had totally gone mad. Of course he said, "uh, yeah, what do you want to go see?" I said, *"The Passion"*. He said, "OK, when do I come and pick you up."

Paul told me later that he got off the phone and started running around like a teenager getting ready for his first date. He even worried about what he would wear. I don't think he had worried about what he would wear since our dating days, and sometimes it was obvious. He came to my door and asked me if I was ready to go.

If you haven't seen *The Passion* because you are afraid of the violence issue, you need to realize that your sin, and my sin caused our Lord to suffer great pain, and it was extremely violent. You need to buy it or rent it today because you need, just as I did, to see what He had to endure for you. I needed a new vision. I needed to see how much He loved me when my sin nailed Him to the cross. So, if He could forgive me, He would give me the strength to forgive Paul (Acceptance stage of grief).

When the movie was over, we were both speechless. When we got back to the car, we just sat there for a minute saying nothing, both of us in tears. Paul took my hand and asked if he could pray. I said, "That would be fine." I don't remember all of his prayer, but he thanked God for His love. He thanked Him for his mercy and he thanked Him for giving his life for us so that we could be freed from the payment of sin. When he finished praying, I prayed one line. "Lord, help me to do what I need to do." I turned to Paul and took his face in my hands and lifted his head. With tears streaming down my face I said, "I forgive you." And then I kissed him. He couldn't even receive my kiss. He was so overcome with emotion that he embraced me and just sobbed.

Throughout many days I cycled through those stages over and over again. I also struggled with having a forgiving heart towards him but God's grace was present each time to be able to release the debt of this sin. I wondered how in the world God was answering my prayer. How was He expanding our borders? How was he going to use this for His glory and our good? Well, it didn't take us long at all to find that out. He has used this and every other horrible circumstance that we have gone through to purify our home, remove those scales, and to expand our borders. I can also say that because of the trials that have come into my life, I am standing before you today, blessed.

Life was hard during those first years after our trauma. We experienced many trials, and spiritual warfare. Debt from ministry and from starting a new business led to financial trauma. We made many stupid mistakes and wrong choices that led us into a huge mess and major captivity. But God has continued to use each and every circumstance in our life to bring glory to Himself.

We went through intensive counseling and learned so much about why we find ourselves in dangerous situations. We learned tools for our marriage that have completely changed the way we relate to each other, our children, and to people we come in contact with every day. But more than anything else, our relationship with our Heavenly Father has changed.
God has grown us up in the faith in so many ways. And because Paul's moral failure, as they called it, was so public, our restoration was as well. Around the second year of our recovery, we began to be asked by other couples who were experiencing their traumas if we could "talk". They began seeking us out to discover how we had received help. We began to encourage and walk with these couples through their own crises and

even helped others escape from potential traumas that were right around the corner.

Finding out about "The Mistress"

Paul and I knew in the first days that we had a long road of recovery ahead of us. If we were going to save our marriage God was going to have to transform it. We talked in confidence to a family member about what happened and they led us to a counselor who worked in sexual addiction and recovery. It was really hard for us to even think about that as a possibility in our marriage! How in the world could we have such issues? We went, grasping at straws, to make our marriage work. We would do whatever it took to find healing.

We went to an intensive workshop and in a nutshell I was labeled a *codependent* and Paul was labeled a *sex addict*. But there was so much more to it than that. The man leading the workshop was named Eli. He helped Paul to see that he had used ministry to feel God's love and acceptance. When ministry was no longer working for him, he used pornography as a way of escape and numbing out. We found that the issues in our marriage were so much bigger than a sexual issue. His cycles of sexual addiction were very far apart because usually ministry, what we now call the "mistress", was his regular place to run to for his escape from pain.

Paul felt such an overwhelming sense of duty to serve God and others that everything else in his life was second, third, or fourth place. His desire to be a great father was also priority over me, so somewhere down the line, I got the leftovers. It was often just enough so this worked for us for eighteen years. We actually had a great ministry, in the world's eyes anyway. I was right there with him as any faithful codependent and enabler should be. We fought throughout the years when I was feeling the pain of being so far down on his list of priorities, but then the shame of not being the "faithful servant" would overtake me and I would "get back in line". I eventually became just as addicted to ministry as he was, so in essence, I allowed the mistress into our home to take residence. How sick is that?

I remember many days that we would fight and I would pack my bags because I was just so wounded by the fact that I didn't have his attention or that I wasn't his priority. But then, I would be so shamed by my selfishness. How dare I desire to be first place! I mean, really? Come on! Ministry and God are the same thing, right? So, I became extremely codependent and this became *"our dance"*, as Eli would describe it. In other words, it was the normal routine of coping for us.

I became accustomed to Paul being gone all the time while living in Honduras. I surrounded myself with activities and relationships to fill my days, when I wasn't right there with him ministering with my music. I was a soprano soloist and recording artist back then. I was the second most requested artist on a radio station on the border of Honduras and El Salvador. I sang in both English and Spanish. I would even be asked to sign autographs and have my picture taken with people. I was "somebody" finally. I felt empowered by the Holy Spirit when I would take the stage and sing. I loved it, yet it was so unfulfilling. Why?

After being back in the USA for a couple of years, I had reverse culture shock. I was no longer "somebody". There were several established soloists in our church and I was not young and fresh any longer here state side. I still had opportunities to sing as we traveled around as missionaries, but as far as someone special, I was not. I really struggled with this for many years. I continually tried to find my value in ministering through music. It was empty and unfulfilling.

Up until then, I never had to ask for opportunities to sing, and it seemed as though if I were going to be able to minister in my own church, I would have to ask. I did find it in myself to ask to be on our church praise team. It was hard. I never felt as though I could measure up, and I couldn't get over my feelings of being a "has been" or unwanted. I eventually stopped singing. I do hope to find the opportunity once again to be able to sing, but for the right reasons and right motivation…and in a safe place.

Chapter THREE

Road to Recovery

When all my kingdoms Fall

Paul was not the only one unfaithful throughout our marriage. A couple of years after being in Honduras and before submerging myself into Paul's addictions like a good co-addict should do (sarcasm implied here), I found myself in compromising circumstances. The first time it happened was over a series of events with our pediatrician in Honduras. He was married, kind, and was very attentive to me.

I needed affirmation and attention so much that as this man made me a priority, I found myself becoming attracted to him. I never acted on this attraction but I looked forward to the house calls he would make to take care of my kids when they were sick. That is so hard for me to admit even to this day. I knew that to act on my fantasy was more than I had in me, so I prayed hard for God to take away the feelings I had. He and his family moved. Thank you Jesus!

The second time was with someone who needed me. Again, I didn't have the guts to act on it so it never went beyond flirtatious conversations. There were never phone calls or any kind of discussions of feelings.

I knew that if I even started to give him an idea that I was available it was all over. I didn't want to lose my marriage or my family, but I was dying inside. I needed attention. I needed to be needed. I needed to be someone's priority.

Neither of these situations was about the man. I can honestly say these men were not the focus. It was about my core needs that were not being met. In both instances while working through the shame, I turned to God, begging Him to take away the emotions, and He did. I finally confessed my unfaithfulness and adulteress thoughts to Paul. I repented and was forgiven. Paul asked for forgiveness that he was not being the husband he needed to be for me. I even became more of a priority to him. It was a bit of a wakeup call for us both.

However, the way for Paul to express his undying love for me… was to include me more in his "affair with the mistress". I started traveling with him again, and we began to minister together. We had visions of having more of an impact together for the kingdom. It was a good desire but with a very unhealthy perspective. And with my Bible studies and cries for God to work in my own heart, He began to work in a mysterious way by allowing my whole world to fall completely apart. All my kingdoms on earth had to be shattered and my dependence on anything and everything else had to fade away.

The Consequences of the Fall

Due to our position, Paul's failure became very public. It was my greatest nightmare to discover that not only had I been very betrayed by my husband, but now I felt betrayal on another level. A letter was sent to over three hundred people explaining that Paul "was caught in a moral failure". This letter went to basically every person in our social world. We had sign-up sheets at churches we visited. I was horrified thinking about the children who had signed up to receive our news letters from churches all across the USA. Then I thought about all the family members I was not regularly in touch with. They would not have known of the biggest mistake of our lives had they not received the letter. I felt like I couldn't breathe.

I remember it like it was yesterday. I found out about the letter as we were driving down Highway 31 in Pelham, Alabama. We had to pull over. I was in a fetal position again and Paul was completely "wigging out" over the pain he had put me through. We couldn't drive and we were both in such agony that all he could do was call our pastor who immediately dropped everything to come to rescue us off the side of the road.

Rumors about this moral failure were quite humorous when we learned about them several years later. We heard everything from Paul having an affair with our maid in Honduras to Elizabeth (our adopted daughter) being his child with another woman. None of which were true. His failure was a onetime occurrence during a layover in route to Albania. He had broken his boundary of leaving the airport and found himself in a compromising situation while viewing the canals of Amsterdam.

But what Satan meant to destroy us, God used for His glory and our good. He always does. I didn't know how God could be working to expand our boarders or bless us in those days. I can honestly say, that although I never want to go through anything like that again, He truly was answering my prayers. Because the moral failure was so public, so was our healing. In our church at first, then even more outside of church.

Several years later our pastor sent a letter of our recovery process and blessing over our ministry to all those that received the first letter. People could see that we not only stuck together but fell in love all over again. We were commissioned to serve the Lord in ministry again. Our worship was more evident and our healing obvious. It was a new start.

Our Underground Ministry

Because our challenges and our healing were so public, it wasn't long before we had our first ministry phone call. "I need help. I was unfaithful to my wife." Then another person, and another, would tap Paul on the shoulder each week and express his need for help.

Men in the church confided to Paul their desire to change their adulterous hearts and women called me with cries for help in their emotions of betrayal. It became what we called our "underground ministry". It was a secret club, so to speak, of people who had marital issues and a desperate desire for help but not exposure.

We ministered like this for nearly four years before ever talking to our church about it. We had one case that was over our heads, and we needed help from our pastor. To his shock, we informed him of how many couples we had helped in the church. He was supportive but desired for us to be healthy and have the covering of the church. As a result we became a vital part of reviving their lay counseling.

We discovered that many times people don't want to go to their own church for help. They are afraid. The church has often been an unsafe place. If caught in a sin in the church, you might be made an example to all. The idea is for the church to be aware and to fear straying from the straight and narrow. But it often becomes a house of judgment and gossip.

Churches sometimes lack the understanding to help individuals who are caught in the pit of sin and deception. Until someone has experienced the pain themselves, it is really hard to help a hurting person.

Many pastors are not equipped to handle these situations because they do not have the training nor a "story", or at least one that others know about.

Pastors, missionaries, and full time Christian workers are terrified to admit they need help, as we were. Confession, as stated in James 5:16, is for healing. We have found that people feel safer with someone who has found healing. They aren't afraid of feeling judged.

After we left our ministry position to find healing, Paul worked a secular job. On the weekends we met with individuals who needed to talk. This went on for a couple of years as God changed our outlook on ministry and healed our lives. God gave us a deeper understanding of who He is, His love, and how to love others and serve God in a healthy way. I felt it was time for full time ministry again. Paul was scared to death and said, "No, I'm not ready." So I waited. I continued to pray and God gave me a vision of what our ministry was going to look like. He began the process of *"expanded boarders and blessing"* as I had prayed from the prayer of Jabez. But God had a lot of work to do in us before that would come to fruition.

Face to Face with the Enemy

Several years into my journey I had a dream. It started out pleasantly. I met a handsome man who seemed kind and peaceful. He did not look threatening at all. I walked up to him to introduce myself, as if I was about to meet a celebrity. In a calm and low voice he said, "I am going to destroy you." I suddenly realized I had been deceived. I knew who he was. I knew how the enemy could disguise himself in a way to catch us off guard, and he knows how to get our attention. I replied to him, "You cannot touch me! I do not belong to you!" He then stated, "I don't have to touch you; I will use others to get to you." Then I woke up. To this day I believe the dream was a warning about events that were about to occur. I am not saying that Satan entered my dreams, because I believe he cannot know or enter our thoughts. But I really felt oppressed by the enemy.

A few days later, we got a call from a friend asking for help. It was another couple whose marriage was in trouble. We had a close relationship with them, so it was devastating to us all. We spent the next week with this couple trying to help them start a process of restoration in their marriage and get the help they needed. The attack from Satan in this couple's marriage touched many wounds in my own heart. I didn't realize they were still so tender, and it resulted in a difficult week for me emotionally and physically.

In the midst of that crisis with our friends we got a call from our former mission agency. They had bad news for us about one of the families we worked with when we served as missionaries. Their daughter had been in a car accident and was brain dead. We immediately left to go see them hours away. The pain that we felt for this family was profound. I have never experienced the grief that we felt for another family like I did when we were with them. The loss of one of my children is one of my biggest fears. This crisis sent me into a major spiral. Fear seemed to take root and grab hold of every ounce of my being.

These two events were the beginning of a series of crises that made my life seem out of control. One of our children became rebellious and I felt powerless at home as a parent. The fear that something horrible would happen to one of my children, because of their own choices, was so overwhelming. The feelings of desperation finally started to spin out of control. I felt powerless to know how to be OK. Satan had clearly examined me very well and knew how to get to me. He knew to use all of my fears, and my wounds of the past. I collapsed into what I understand now to have been an emotional breakdown. And he didn't have to touch me at all….he used those I loved.

I believed that I had been trusting in God and His power, but I now realize that I often trusted in my own strength and in the knowledge I had of Scriptures to help me to resist the enemy. Well, it didn't work! I realized clearly that sometimes there is not near enough strength in me to fight Satan on my own. And no matter how many scriptures I recited, it wouldn't help me to fight this enemy. I had to come to the end of myself and surrender to God. I had to trust Him to control what I could not control. I had to recognize that

God allows things to happen to us that are out of our control. Sometimes we will not understand until we see Him face to face, but He will use these things to bring us closer to Him and to deepen our faith. He also uses them to enable us to minister to others through our experiences.

Chapter FOUR

Emotional Flooding

My Battle with Rage

With this emotional breakdown I completely fell apart. I wanted Paul to fix things that were out of control. I was looking to him to make it all better. He also could not control the events going on in our life at that time. I was making him out to be a god instead of looking to my heavenly Father for help. My life was unmanageable and I blamed Paul. It reached a point where I ended up on the bathroom floor screaming and crying, "I just want to die!" Paul opened the door and saw me watching blood run down my hand where I cut it on a vase that I broke in a rage when we were in a fight. At that moment he realized he had to get me help.

Paul phoned some ladies from our church who came straight over to our house. They asked me questions and I could not remember the events that had just occurred. I did not remember what I had said or what I had done. I wasn't even certain how I cut myself. Paul told one of the ladies what happened, and as she repeated it to me the events came back to memory, but were so shameful. I was told I needed a break. Paul and the kids would need to leave the house or I needed to leave. I knew I could refuse, but that would be completely selfish and even more destructive to my kids. Regardless, I really had no choice legally because I had hit Paul during the fight and therefore could have been arrested.

One of the ladies took me to someone's home. I spent two weeks as a guest of one of our pastors and his family. His wife took great care of me. She did not treat me as someone crazy or horrible but with complete love and compassion. I still felt so much shame and despair.

I was also told I needed to see a licensed psychologist and I did. He told me something that I will forever be grateful for. He said, "You are not crazy, you have two feet fully planted on the ground, you just lack the confidence in who you are and I will help you get there." He started focusing on all the things in my world that I was good at. I wasn't being told I didn't measure up. Some counselors would blame the family of origin in situations like this, but he did not focus there. He focused on my beliefs about myself that I had developed over the years. He began pouring into me each session that I was a strong and capable individual but had faulty thinking.

As Paul and I met with this psychologist, things were exposed in our relationship. I realized I was being beat down and then lifted up, leaving me feeling completely helpless. One session I was asked to leave the room. I have since heard that Paul was "chewed out" by him.

He said, "Do you realize you are completely destroying your wife with your words? You speak death on her continually!" Paul began to wake up to the fact that he was not innocent in this at all. He realized he was playing into my insecurities. He felt it his responsibility to always make me okay and I didn't like it. I no longer wanted him to play the role of being my god.

Codependency is the need to make someone else okay so that you can be okay. Enmeshment is the lack of any boundaries with others. What happens is two people are all in each other's business and one (sometimes both) loses their identity, either by force or manipulation or simply giving it away. We were two very codependent and enmeshed individuals. This often caused me to spiral into rage because I believed that unless Paul agreed with me on any issue that was important to me, that I could not be alright. Since I felt I was right in whatever was important to me, I had to continue to convince him until he changed his mind.

Yet to win seemed very empty and shameful, and it felt like he was just giving in to end the fight. If I did not have extreme conviction in an argument, I would typically back down sooner to 'submit', and feel like my voice was completely squashed, and unheard. I felt like a horrible wife either way because so much shame came from not being that "meek and quiet spirit" in our relationship.

When one or the other has to be right, someone always loses. And mainly the relationship loses. What we have learned through recovery is to understand the heart behind our differences and respect that our individual opinions always matter. And it is okay to disagree about situations and thoughts. If there needs to be a compromise, we work on it from the standpoint of trying to understand the heart underneath. Trusting that your spouse is not against you, but is for you, is the key to ending this crazy cycle.

Anger is not a Primary Emotion

One of the things that my psychologist helped me to see is that there is always emotion under my anger. I was urged to avoid anger at any cost in the beginning and to take time out and leave the uncomfortable situation before I got angry. My meltdown happened right before all the holidays. All four of our children were home for Christmas. The two oldest were in college at the time. It has always been hard to play games as a family because we are all so competitive. If we were losing, we would get angry. This particular evening we were playing a game as a family. Paul and the boys started arguing. I began to feel the heat rising in me and it was uncomfortable, so I left the room without saying anything. This disrupted the game and everyone seemed frustrated with me. But, I did not allow their hurt towards me to stop me from doing what I had to do for myself.

This event, I believe, was the first time I recognized my need and stood up for myself and said, "If I stay here, I will explode on someone". As they were fussing and stating the rule of "no one leaves the game", I said, "I do not deserve to settle for using anger to express my emotions. I need a time out so that I do not react in anger." I allowed them to not be okay with me. I deserved better. Wow! I didn't have to get my value from them. I could get that from myself by allowing God to help me see I deserved better. That was the first time in my life that I defended my own heart without attacking anyone else. It felt great and empowering!

Part of my therapy for my emotional healing was exercise. I was told to keep from being hospitalized and put on medication, I needed to exercise every day. Exercise raises the *endorphins* and helps with mental stability and clear thinking. I was very interested in the connection between unhealthy eating, depression, sex addiction, and anger addiction. Fast forward now a few years. I began studying psychology and Christian counseling. When I started, my desire was to become a life coach. I was bored with exercising by myself and wanted to be with other women. I wrote a bible study and healthy eating program called *Freedom Finders*.

I had no idea how to get this out to others and no real platform any longer now that we were no longer in ministry. I talked to the pastors at my church and shared with them the study and they agreed to allow me to teach this program to ladies. About this same time, I began to feel God strongly leading me to coach other women who struggled with depression, anxiety and such. I placed an ad on Craig's List for volunteers for a study. I called it "Walking and Talking". I received phone calls from several women (I would not walk with a man so the ad was for Christian women only). These women were great. I ended up walking and talking, with about six different women.

To this day I still keep in touch with three of them. God opened my eyes to how connected our negative thoughts and pain from the past are with the strongholds that control us. These strongholds are actually messages we receive from painful events that happen throughout our lives. Everything we think about will be filtered through these messages. The reality is these messages are not truths. They are lies that the devil has spoken about us and we have embedded them into our subconscious minds and deep into our hearts.

The first time I heard in my Christian Counseling courses that anger was not a primary emotion many things suddenly became clear to me. I had never looked at it that way. I would use "angry" as one of my feeling words all the time. But there is always something under the anger that makes us angry. When I was dealing with Post Traumatic Stress Disorder (PTSD) after a car wreck, my psychologist taught me how to breathe and refocus my thoughts. I started doing this when I felt angry as well. This allowed me the time to focus on what was beneath the anger. I watched Gary Oliver's video on the primary emotions, which are hurt, unmet expectations or frustrations, and fear and anxiety (sometimes we can experience all of those in some form or fashion) and it totally rocked my world.

Until I understood these primary emotions, all I could feel was the anger. Focusing on the anger would never allow me to find the healing I needed to bring about the change. When I realized that I could use the breathing techniques that were taught to combat PTSD to slow down everything and refocus, it allowed me to identify core emotions and stop reacting by lashing out or shutting down. I started to express my true emotions, which helped my husband and others to understand me better. It also gave me the confidence that I needed to stand with my two feet firmly planted on the ground.

I am now teaching this technique to women and men struggling with anger or anxiety. Understanding what is below the anger is the primary way to change your world. I also recognized that my feelings are valid. Even if they are not accurate according to those around me, they are always valid to me. My feelings come from filtered thinking and a belief system that I have that is unique only to me. We are all that way. Because of the beliefs we have about ourselves, about God, and about others, we respond through feelings and emotions that originate with these message filters.

If I can recognize what I believe about myself, about God, or about others, I am able to back track and determine the lie from the enemy and the truth according to the Gospel of Jesus Christ. Philippians 4 is my favorite passage of scripture because of what it teaches about the mind. The mind is where all strongholds, addictions, and anger begin. If we can take a moment and stop to measure what we are thinking about with the truth of God's Word, then we are able to work through conflict with others without explosive anger.

Taking *time outs* was crucial to my recovery and has been the saving grace for many others with whom I now work. One other study we found while writing material for our workshops was *Emotional Flooding*. We also refer to it as emotionally spiraling. When I stopped reacting to the urge to lash out or respond, but instead took a time out of at least twenty minutes to cool down, it became easier to control my anger.

Studies of the brain show that it takes twenty minutes for endorphins to slow down and get back in check. When you get angry your heart rate increases, your blood pressure rises, you become agitated. You can easily turn to rage, or simply shut down. Both responses to anger are equally destructive to a relationship. Many think that the outwardly explosive and loud individual is the problem in a relationship. But as I began to stop my explosive behavior, Paul's implosive and passive aggressive behavior was exposed. If there is an explosive person in a relationship there is usually an implosive person who becomes a victim, and the explosive becomes the monster. In reality, both of these ways of dealing with anger can completely destroy a marriage relationship.

Dealing with anger and expressing my emotions in a healthier way was key to my husband learning to express his emotions in a non-threatening and non-passive aggressive way. One of the ways that we teach this is through Chip Ingram's Anger ABCD:

Acknowledge my anger.

Backtrack to my primary emotion.

Consider the cause.

Direct the right response.

Mad about Us:
 Moving from Anger to Intimacy with Your Spouse
      by Gary J. Oliver, Carrie Oliver Baker Books, 2007

Conclusion of *PART ONE*

As I look back at my story, I have to celebrate the new life God has given me and the transformation that came from all of the chaos. One of the most hopeful things I learned was that **chaos can be the doorway to intimacy**. When Paul and I have experienced chaos in our relationship, it has been the beginning of change, and change brought about tremendous blessings. In the middle of the storms we would never be able to see that, but now looking back, God was removing the imperfections that were destroying us. I could continue to tell you things that God had to strip away from us to bring about change, but I will just end it by saying….He's still not done with us yet.

Part of celebrating our restored relationship came by renewing our marriage vows a year after our journey began. We sent out invitations to all those who received the bad news to be a part of the good news of God's redeeming work in our lives and in our marriage. It was a beautiful reflection of grace.

As I reflect on how God prepared me to walk through the valley, and then was with me through the storms, I can rejoice in the fact that I was never left alone. He continued to bring people into my life who would love me by speaking hard truth to me and helping us see the things that were unhealthy in our marriage. Without His hands and feet, we would not be where we are today. Without the storms of life, the chaos, we would not have changed. I am thankful. And as we have been comforted, my hope is that you are comforted as well.

My friend, there is HOPE!

PART TWO

Restoration of a Dark Heart

by Paul C. Talley Sr.

Introduction

There will be some overlap with my story and Suzanne's, but this is important to help you put all the pieces together. I will look more in-depth at my childhood. It is important to do so to expose my faulty thinking, and the lies I believed about God, myself, and others for the first forty years of my life. My desire is to be open about my faulty thinking, the depths of my sins, to give you a doorway into my darkness so that you might find hope for your life.

Some of the events of my life might be shocking to some, but they are not meant to be offensive in any way. They are written for explanation and not as an excuse for my behavior. Writing about how I felt during certain events in my life is not meant to reflect on anyone's motivation, especially my family and close friends through the years.

One of the things I say today in helping men and couples on almost a daily bases is **"your feelings are valid but your conclusions might not be."** This statement is applicable to introduce my story. To let you in, I must share what I was feeling at the time. In no way am I saying that all of my conclusions were correct. When dealing with feelings, or learning to deal with feelings, we often think that, if my feelings are valid then my conclusions determined by those feelings must be right as well. Nothing could be further from the truth.

One of the biggest signs of emotional maturity is the ability to own your feelings and communicate them, if needed, and then release the outcome. On the other hand, in emotional immaturity we try to ignore our feelings, stuff them, or if we share them we have a predetermined idea how they should be received. Emotional maturity really is seen and true joy and inner peace are found in releasing what someone will do, say or think about those feelings. I call that releasing of the results, releasing the conclusions. May it be understood that the biggest battle is not releasing the results of others but inwardly fighting yourself not to make conclusions at all.

Again my purpose for writing is to bring hope and encouragement and not destruction or discouragement in any way to those who are part of my story.

May God bless you and encourage you, and give you hope as you read.

Chapter FIVE

Loneliness and Shame

My First Emotions

I was raised in a Christian home as the youngest of three boys. When I was born, my dad was in his last year of his M.Div. at *Grace Theological Seminary* in Warsaw, Indiana. Upon graduation, he joined the Army and we moved to Augusta, Georgia. He entered into the US Army to be a Chaplain and go to Vietnam to minister to the men on the front lines. I was three years old when he left, four when he returned, and do not have any memory of those events. Soon after his return my mom got pregnant. But because my father was on the front lines most of his term he had *Agent Orange* dumped on him repeatedly. Consequently, my baby brother, Timothy, died from multiple birth defects and lived less than 24 hours.

My earliest memories stem from this time. My family can testify that I don't have the best memory and I don't remember much of my early childhood except for feelings of deep loneliness and shame. I am sure family and friends were all around me, but I can only remember being all alone and ashamed.

I was told that my behavior changed at home and at school for a while, but I don't remember those details. In a book my mom wrote called, *Paul's Guilt*, I learned that I felt guilty (we would say "shame". See *Chapter 13- Guilt or Shame*) that Timothy died because I didn't want a baby brother - I wanted to continue being the baby! It goes on to explain how I went through all the stages of grief but eventually got back to "normal", whatever that is for a four/five year old kid that just survived a huge family trauma.

It is unbelievable, but soon after this tragic loss the Army wanted my dad to return back to Vietnam immediately. He asked for an extension of time from the Pentagon but they refused to give it. My dad was well decorated in his term in Vietnam and wanted to fulfill his lifetime goal to be a career military man. But because my mom was still very sick and grieving he felt he had no other choice but to leave the Army and depart from his dream.

After he left the Army, we moved to Dayton, Ohio so that he could become a pastor. We lived there for three years. Sadly I don't have many good memories of that time in Dayton. The few good vague memories were playing kick ball in the cul-de-sac, playing center for my brothers football games in the back yard with my dad, and playing cards with the curtains shut (because cards were seen as a sin by some in the church).

My clear memories are more negative ones. I remember being caught helping my brothers steal cigarettes to smoke with the deacon's kids, and feeling the shame and disappointment that we brought to our parents when we were caught. I also remember my bike locking up and flying over the handle bars, having my teeth busted out, being rushed to the hospital, and having to wear a mouth piece to school. I remember being teased and made fun of for that mouth piece. It made me feel different, weird, and alone again.

In the middle of my third grade year we moved to Covington, Virginia for my dad to be the head pastor of another church. I learned as an adult that after just several weeks he knew that he had made a mistake. I was told he felt God calling him to go back to school to get his Doctorate while he was in Dayton, but he resisted that calling. He believed God calling him ultimately to teach at a Bible College training pastors.

So after just six months in Covington, we moved again to Portland, Oregon so that dad could go back to school and earn his doctorate. Nine months later, he was asked to become a professor at Appalachian Bible Institute (now College) in Beckley, West Virginia, so once again we moved. That was clearly the right decision for him, as he taught at three different Bible Colleges, and was a professor, department head, academic dean, vice president, president, and then retired as a professor after I was married and had my own family.

When I was a child we obviously moved around a lot as my dad followed God's leading to different ministries. I was always the new kid in class and felt alone, different, and weird; not to mention I was the preacher's kid or the son a of a Bible College professor. It seemed I was always making new friends. I felt different and awkward, and I didn't like those feelings. I learned to morph into a person that people would like and accept. I felt that being Paul was not good enough because I had nothing exciting to offer, or because I was weird and different. As a result I became a chronic liar. It is a very lonely, shameful, and painful place as a chronic liar.

Some of my best memories were of growing up in West Virginia. I made good friends living on campus, where married students had kids my age. The campus was covered with woods that we could explore. The winters were full of good times sledding and inter-tubing on the snow. In the summer we skinny dipped in the pond when camp was not in session. But it was also a place of loneliness as my brothers had their friends and I had mine. Little boys yearn for acceptance from their older brothers. I desperately wanted to be part of their lives, not just some of the time, but all of the time. Unfortunately I was the punk little brother.

In our first home in West Virginia I had a separate bedroom from my older brothers for the first time that I could remember. Up to this point, we had always shared a room. But there I slept in my own room, which was also the guest room, so it never felt like mine. I also didn't like sleeping alone. I have been teased most of my life that I was spoiled, and one of the examples that is used is me having my own room.

West Virginia is known for heavy thunderstorms and at that time I was very frightened by them. One night I asked my brothers during a storm if I could sleep in their room. They got mad at me and told me to go away. I wanted to run to my parent's room but for some reason I felt that I couldn't go there (today we call that an *unspoken rule*) so I didn't. The storm continued and I returned a second time telling my brothers I would sleep on the floor, but please let me sleep in their room. They laughed at me and told me to get out.

When I returned to my room I pulled the covers over my head and placed all the pillows on top of me. That night I began a life of fantasy. When I didn't feel safe I would go somewhere else to feel safe. I imagined that night that I was riding in the back of a truck. I imagined that the fear I felt was not from the thunder storm but fear of being discovered in the truck. I had to be quiet and breathe lightly so I would not be discovered. It worked and I fell asleep. I used that technique often over the next several years, and it opened my mind to a new world of escaping. I felt alone and I had to take care of myself, because I believed that no one else would.

When I was in the sixth grade we still lived in West Virginia. About the age of ten or eleven, in one of my escape times, I discovered masturbation. I didn't even know what I was doing because I never had a sex talk that I could remember or at least understand. But I knew I had found another place where I could escape and feel good, and feeling good wasn't something I was very familiar with. I was so unaware of what I was doing and what potentially would happen. I remember being a little scared when I ejaculated for the first time. I very quickly began to enjoy taking a bath, which I think pleased my parents because I was at least clean. I was known and teased for my "stinky feet", so taking a bath was good for eliminating that odor. To this day I still don't like taking off my shoes, even though my feet do not stink anymore.

The next year I changed schools again as I went off to Junior High. All those same feelings presented themselves again, as I was in a small one room school house for grade school and then went to a very large school for Junior High. That year I was jumped from behind and beat up. I was walking from the gym back to the main building and a guy in my P.E. class began to hit me before I even knew what was happening. I remember feeling all alone as everyone just sat and watched that happened. This guy rode my bus and was one of the "Sand Branch kids" that lived near the Bible College. I always felt afraid of them. This guy had failed several years and was much older, probably the age of my brothers and a lot bigger.

I couldn't understand why he attacked me, but somehow knew it had to do with me being one of the Bible College kids. I feared him, always looking over my shoulder for months. One morning while waiting outside for the school doors to open he jumped me again. As he punched my face I fell to the ground, and then something happened that I will never forget. One of the fellow Bible College kids named Bob stepped in and pulled him off me. He slammed him up against the school building and said, "Leave Paul alone or you will have to deal with me." Bob was huge for his age. So huge he died at a young age with heart failure. I remember when I heard the news that he died something died inside of me, but I wouldn't tell anyone. That day I felt good to be protected and valued by Bob. But I also hurt as I wondered why I wasn't protected and valued by my big brothers that were standing there with me. I felt alone and not good enough to be protected by my brothers.

That same year I was exposed to pornography by some older friends from my brothers' group, who brought clippings out of magazines to a tree house. I wasn't able to get a clear look because the bigger kids wouldn't allow me and my friends to see. Over the next several years I ran across similar pictures several times walking through the woods. The response from my body and my emotions was amazing. I was always on the lookout because I wanted to see what the bigger kids saw. When I did find some pictures, I always felt special and accepted. I began to have a different type of escape in the bathtub, as the pornography and my fantasy world merged, making it even more enjoyable.

The summer of my eighth grade year, my dad was asked to return to Southeastern Bible College in Birmingham, Alabama, where he had studied prior to earning his M.Div. at *Grace Theological Seminary*. So we moved again. I was in the eighth grade. I can remember sitting in science class the first semester like it was yesterday. The class was full of cheerleaders and athletes. I sat there again by myself with no one talking to me, and I decided I was going to be someone. I was not going to be a "nobody" anymore. I needed to become popular, but I was not sure how to do it.

Around that time, I saw my first full pornographic magazine under the bed of my oldest brother. I was hooked! It did something in me that was indescribable. I felt special, wanted, and accepted by all those pictures. I had never seen so many at one time. I was overwhelmed by that one magazine, but even more so when I saw that there were many to choose from.

I became consumed with planning how to sneak into my brother's bedroom in the basement, get one of the magazines, go to the bathroom upstairs, masturbate, and get it back without being discovered. I was never caught, and that was a thrill on many different levels. I had lost control and didn't even realize it. When my brother was home and in his room, I would get upset waiting for him to leave so I could sneak in again. I developed a dark secret in my life that no one could know.

Being raised in a Christian and Pastor's/Professor's home, I knew that it was wrong and felt ashamed, but my desire for that feeling always overshadowed my shame. My brother graduated from high school, moved out and my "fix" was gone. I was constantly on the lookout. I found magazines in the woods and on the road, and when I couldn't stand it anymore, I would stoop to buying one. The desire for the escape, thrill, the rush, and the excitement sometimes was unbearable, and I had to have it. I was out of control but I had to keep this secret to myself.

Chapter SIX

I Want To Be Someone!

My #1 Desire

The second semester of my eighth grade year I decided I needed to become an athlete to gain popularity and acceptance. I tried out and made the Hewitt-Trussville Jr. High varsity football team that spring. I was named the starting tight-end for the spring game, and then for the ninth grade. People took notice. The cheerleaders and athletes knew who I was and even talked to me. Thursdays were game days, and I felt special because we were allowed to wear our football jerseys to school. I felt people looking at me, accepting me, and it felt good.

I also tried out for the Jr. High varsity basketball team and made the team as the starting point guard. Without my football helmet on people recognized me even more. One of the cheerleaders became my girlfriend. In my mind I had arrived ... then came high school. I had to start all over again as the new kid on the block. I continued to play sports in high school and made the JV football and basketball teams.

That summer I got a job at the *Der Wienerschnitzel* in Center Point, Alabama. I quickly rose to the position of night time shift manager. I was about fifteen and boss over coworkers that were sixteen to twenty. I was somebody, I had money, and I was in charge. Life felt good.

When I worked on Saturdays I got to know a twenty year old coworker who worked the day shift. She lived close by and after a while offered to take me home after work. Then she got her schedule changed to work some nights. It was obvious that she liked me, and even better, she was a woman and I was no more than fifteen!

One night when she was taking me home, she went a different way and pulled down a dark road. I asked what she was doing and she just said, "You will see". She parked the car and pushed me to engage with her sexually. What we were doing felt good, but it was scary because I didn't know what to do. I knew I couldn't show her my fear but I felt weird, awkward, and alone all over again. She continued, I didn't know what was happening, and don't even remember everything that did happen. I do remember that I didn't perform to her standards.

She pushed me away, and drove me home. I felt rejected and awkward. I sat in silence the rest of the way home. When we got to my house, I wanted to talk about it but instead she reached over me and opened the door. I repeated that I wanted to talk and at that point she pushed me out of her car onto the ground. As I laid there face down to the ground, I could smell the grass and the damp soil from the dew that had already fallen. That smell still resonates to this day. I rolled over and began to cry still not sure what had happened.

I was worried. What if she was pregnant? I couldn't sleep that night. The next day I went to work looking for her so we could talk. She didn't want to talk. I asked her if she was pregnant and she laughed at me and told me I was crazy or stupid. That crushed me, and once again I felt awkward, weird, and alone. I also felt inadequate.

Before Christmas break of that year a popular senior girl at school noticed me and we started a relationship. The senior guys hated me and I loved every minute of it. I was somebody even to those who hated me! We dated for over a year and a half.

In high school I discovered that being an athlete was not enough to advance my popularity. I didn't like that feeling. The popular crowd also went to parties, drank, and used drugs, so I joined in. I didn't like beer but drank it to be accepted. Then I was introduced to marijuana and liked it, so I ditched the beer. Marijuana became my drug of choice.

My girlfriend was old enough to get into bars so we could go dancing, drink, and have fun. That is when I discovered Jack and Coke. I partied pretty hard for several years and then she went off to college. So now here I am a junior in high school and dating a college girl. I felt like the big man on campus. That year I was voted most popular in the junior class, and named as a starter for the varsity football team - one of only two juniors to accomplish that. I was special.

The second game of the season I dislocated my knee and was out for the rest of the season. The manager took me to the doctor because I had no family there at the game. This was the only game since starting football that someone from my family was not there. As I sat in the back seat of his car I could feel my dream of popularity slipping away, and once more I was consumed with loneliness.

My girlfriend wanted to have sex and we had tried several times over the year and a half that we dated. Something always went wrong because I didn't know what I was doing, so it never happened. That frustrated her. Then we broke up when I discovered she had been with a college guy. She claimed nothing happened, that she was sorry, and wanted to work it out. But I didn't want to feel this way anymore. I hated not being enough. My world was crashing in on me.

I started to smoke marijuana frequently by myself. It was an escape to a new level. I skipped school a lot because I didn't care. Marijuana made me not worry what people thought of me. I kept partying and that fueled my feelings of acceptance.

I got sick one night at home after drinking cheap wine at a party. My grandparents were visiting and my grandmother told my parents she heard me sick in the bathroom. My father talked to me and gave me an ultimatum. If I continued to live that way I would have to leave their house. I tried to cover up with a lie. "I drank some bad tea," I told him. He wasn't buying it. To survive at home I hid the way I was living even better. I didn't drink much from that time forward, but smoked marijuana even more, because it didn't make me sick. I could cover my tracks better with marijuana than with alcohol.

Then spring break came and the whole family was leaving for vacation. I convinced my parents I had to work, so they allowed me to stay home. I called in sick every day and stayed drunk or high from marijuana for a week. Two of my friends came over and spent spring break with me. We partied and we had girls over several times. My friends were successful having sex but I was not. "What was wrong with me?" I thought.

My oldest brother, who had turned his life over to the Lord during his freshman year of college, came home early from spring break, before I could get the house completely cleaned up. We had removed all the big things like beer cans and alcohol bottles. He had been asking me to go to church with him for a while but I was not interested.

I was not there when my brother arrived. Before he left he made a pile of all the evidence he could find - marijuana roaches, beer tabs, etc. When I returned, I was shocked to see the pile of evidence, and thought I was going to be kicked out of the house. About an hour later he came back to the house and said nothing about the pile, but simply asked if I wanted to go to church with him the next day. I said "yes!" I would do anything to keep him happy at that point. That night I felt empty and scared, and uncertain what was going to happen to me. Was he going to tell my parents? Did my parents already know? I thought about how I had lived for the past week. I felt an emptiness come over me like never before. I had achieved my goal to be popular, but I still felt empty, inadequate, and all alone.

The next day my brother picked me up for church. He was the youth pastor there and took me to Sunday school. Then we went to the church service. I don't remember the sermon at all, but after the service they had communion. The pastor emphasized not to take communion in an "unworthy way". When I was five or six, everyone in my house were Christians. I realized that and I didn't like being different so I prayed a salvation prayer. I felt accepted and everyone was happy with me, but was I truly saved then?

For the first time since I prayed that prayer I didn't take communion, because I knew how I was living and was not sure I was truly a Christian. Later that day, my oldest brother talked to me about how I could know if I was a Christian. So the second semester of my junior year of High School, at the age of seventeen, I gave myself completely to the Lord. I even surrendered my life to full-time ministry that same month. My problem was solved, my emptiness was gone!

The day after I gave my life to the Lord I returned back to school. Everyone was talking about what they did over spring break. Everyone that went to the beach heard about the party at the Talley's house and began to ask, "What's next....where's the party going to be this weekend?" I told them I was a Christian now and was not going to party anymore. They laughed at me, made fun of me, and I felt very alone.

Two days after spring break I was called to the vice-principal's office and was told I was being expelled from school for truancy and other things I don't remember. But I do remember the panic I felt. I rushed to the Bible College to tell my dad, hopefully before the school called him. When I arrived, I didn't know my dad already knew, so I struggled to tell him the truth. It was hard because I hadn't been truthful about anything for a long time. He let me struggle and I told him. It was one of the hardest things I had ever done but it felt good.

My dad did something that day that I will never forget. He said, "It's ok," and that he thought it was Satan trying to defeat me and not to get discouraged. Wow, my dad wasn't kicking me out of the house! He also said that he had worked things out with the vice principal and I wasn't expelled, just suspended, and he wanted me to enjoy a couple of days off from school. I couldn't believe my ears. I felt love and acceptance from my dad like never before.

My dad told me that day why I was named Paul. His prayer since I was born was for me to become a missionary, like the Apostle Paul, and that intrigued me. I returned to school later that week, and when I walked down the halls it felt like the parting of the Red Sea as people moved away from me because they heard that I had become a Christian. The awkward feelings of inadequacy and loneliness came rushing back again.

That semester I felt like I really only had one male friend. His name was Mike. He had struggled through high school trying to figure out who he wanted to be, alternating between partying and living for God. He was a great encouragement to me and I don't think I would have made it through that year without him.

By the time my junior year album came out the person pictured under the caption "Most Favorite" had only one true male friend. At times I would return to masturbation and occasionally pornography to feel better, but now I didn't just think it was wrong, I was being convicted by the Holy Spirit that it was wrong, and I would run to God. It felt good to feel God's cleansing power over my life. But sometimes it also felt very lonely because no one else knew about it.

Throughout my senior year I grew spiritually but I also struggled with my dark secret. It was not like before but it was still there. I was so thankful to God that He was there and He understood me and accepted me. It felt good to be accepted just the way I was. But there was a problem. God understood, but nobody else knew. If they knew I believed I would not be accepted in the church. I felt unwelcome alone in a place where you are supposed to feel welcome. I had to morph into what I was expected to be in the church, not be truthful with what I was struggling with, and live a lie. The sense of failure was suffocating.

As my struggle with sin continued, my guilt turned into shame about who I was or who I wasn't. When I felt the conviction of the Holy Spirit, instead of running to God, I hid in shame, as Adam did in the Garden of Eden. I wanted to talk to someone about it but I was afraid I would be rejected. I thought nobody would understand, nobody is like me, nobody struggles like me. Or they would understand and tell me I really wasn't a Christian, or that Christian's don't do things like that.

Often I would ask myself "Am I really a Christian?" This was a difficult time in my life and during this time the roots of me hiding as a Christian took hold. I was living a double life and knew that my secret sin had to be contained more than ever. I couldn't let anyone know and I had to fix this myself. All those feelings that I had felt all my life started to come back but this time it was different. I always felt like I was doing something bad, but then I began to believe that I am something bad. The weight was heavy. I had to do something about this. I had to get this fixed before I was discovered.

Chapter SEVEN

True Happiness

Can I truly find it?

After my high school graduation, I went to Southeastern Bible College to learn about God, know Him more deeply, and prepare to serve Him full-time. I learned how to study the Bible and pray effectively, and grew closer to God. I struggled less throughout my freshmen year of Bible College with sexual lust and it felt good.

My dad encouraged me to consider missions, and as a result I traveled to Honduras and stayed for a month with a missionary there. I did this for two summers. I shared my testimony to high schoolers and many got saved. The rush, the thrill, and the acceptance I felt was better than any drugs or pornography. I was on fire for God. I had found what I was looking for. I had found the missing piece!

I returned to Southeastern Bible College and to my surprise other students were uncomfortable for my zeal to serve God on the mission field. Girls were afraid to date me because they knew if the relationship continued they would be going to a far off land to live in a "mud hut". I began to feel weird, awkward, out of place, and all alone all over again. To my shame, my dark secret began to show its ugly head again. It was still there and I was depressed. Even when I didn't act out it was a constant battle to keep it away because those negative feelings were so strong. It would get exhausting at times and I would give in and not fight it anymore.

When I gave in to temptation the rush was great. The thrill and the peace lasted for a moment, and then I would crash. Oh the shame I would feel! It exposed itself during those college years with magazines, visits to an adult bookstore downtown, and fondling with girls on dates. I even went to strip clubs a couple of times. But mostly I would escape the pressure with masturbation in my dorm room with old images stored in my head. I knew looking at pornography and doing those other things were wrong. I tried to use my Bible study skills to prove it was okay to masturbate, but without success. I felt like if I knew God more it would help rid me of my dark secret completely, but it never did.

During the summer of my junior year of college I formally met Suzanne. I had seen her at church several times. She was a soloist and she sang like an angel. I began working for her dad and got to know her. We started to date. On our third date, I popped the question, well not the BIG question but it a was question I feared the most at the time. I asked her if she was willing to go to the mission field and she said something interesting; "I will go wherever God leads my husband." Wow. In a strange way I felt accepted. I fell deeply in love with her quickly, and so the next year, a week after graduation from Bible College, we got married.

Finally my problem was solved; my lustful sin would go away. No, I just was convicted more, which led to more shame and now more risk of losing someone I deeply cared about, if she found out. The struggle was less at the beginning, maybe because of the newness of marriage, wanting to be a godly husband, and probably our active sex life, but soon none of that was enough. I excused myself by thinking she didn't understand my needs.

During the first year of marriage, I worked a full-time job for an asphalt/concrete company, became pastor of a local church, and raised support to go on the mission field. The youngest person in that church was around fifty and I was just twenty four, but they looked to me to lead them, feed them spiritually, and grow the church. Again I felt the rush and the thrill of being accepted. But they didn't really know me and if they did it would all come crumbling down.

My life was very busy, so I just didn't have a lot of time for my secret sin and that felt good. Through my busyness, I was able to distance myself from it for most of the year, but toward the end of that year several things happened. First, I was just plain exhausted from everything I was doing. In addition, the church wasn't growing, and neither was our support to go to the mission field. Support came in very slowly and I felt like God was punishing me because He knew me. So, I welcomed back my "faithful friend" for the thrill, the rush and calmness that it could bring me for a moment.

Then I would wake up from the fog back to reality and the shame would hit me; you're a pastor, you're going to the mission field, you're a husband. Are you crazy or stupid? There were those words again. The same words the twenty year old girl hit me with when I went to ask if she was pregnant.

Then in a short amount of time things changed. I thought, "Was God giving me another chance?" We had our first baby, finally got all our financial support in, and were able to leave for a year of language school in Costa Rica. I was so excited to be in Latin America again and in language school. I was finally feeling a sense of fulfillment, and if I was fulfilled, lustful temptation and sin would go away.

We rented a house in Costa Rico that came with cable. It had HBO and Cinemax. I was exposed to something new. Now it wasn't merely pictures - it was on TV. We would be watching a show or movie containing "soft" porn (nudity) in the middle of the day. I thought, "If this was on now what would it be at night?" To my shame, a couple of times, I would watch at night the more explicit stuff while Suzanne was sleeping. I am glad our house was small and Suzanne was around a lot or it could have been worse.

I became sick and it grew worse. I finally went to the doctor and was diagnosed with Hepatitis NonA/NonB (now known as Hep C). I thought that God was punishing me once again because He knew me and I deserved it. He knew what I had looked at even after He had given me another chance. Suzanne was tested as well and the doctor said it was a negative/positive. What did that mean? She was negative to Hepatitis but was positive to being pregnant....I thought, "She is pregnant!"

The doctor explained to us that with Hepatitis NonA/NonB it could be more like Hepatitis A, which is more like Mononucleosis. It lasts about a month and then is gone. Or it could be more like Hepatitis B which could be fatal over time and he didn't know what type it was. He advised us that I should be quarantined from my wife and my son.

Suzanne slept in a separate bedroom. I had my own plate and silverware that no one else could use. Our son PJ would bang on my bedroom door because he wanted to see his daddy. I felt that I was letting everyone down. I couldn't be there for my wife or my son because of my sin. What I was hearing was that it is better for people to stay away from me or I would infect them. As I look back, I had always felt that, because I was weird, different and awkward. Now I was isolated. Several days later, we had to leave Costa Rica so that I could get medical attention in the States.

I got a little better, gained some strength, and we returned to Costa Rica. I felt like I needed to prove to God I could do this, and then He would be proud of me. I wanted to be able to have the rush and thrill of helping people like I did on my summer mission trips and as a pastor. Suzanne developed problems with her pregnancy and had to return to the States, but I stayed. I had to, because if I could get to Honduras as a missionary and be fulfilled, then with that fulfillment I could finally release my dark secret forever. Just two weeks later, I was asked to come home because there were even bigger problems.

When I arrived back home to the States, I was told that our second baby had major complications. He was diagnosed with *Hydrocephalus*, which is water on the brain. We were told he could be born blind and/or deformed with many complications. The pain I felt inside and the shame was overwhelming. I thought I was still being punished by God because of my sin and now it was hurting people around me again. He couldn't or wouldn't use me.

I called our director and told him, "My dream of going overseas is over, but maybe God could use me here in the States some day." I was devastated, depressed, and very ashamed. We prayed together, asked many others to pray as well, and God did something miraculous.

After just three days in the NICU, our son Benjamin was released with a clean bill of health! What was God doing? Was he giving me another chance? Could I finally find the happiness that I had been looking for all my life?

Chapter EIGHT

Battling My Dark Secret!

The Mistress of Ministry

We were finally released after getting a clean bill of health for Benjamin. We had raised the additional support we thought we needed to go to Honduras to serve the Lord and find fulfillment. Hopefully my problems were solved. Instead, things got worse. Now I was in a foreign country, with very little language skills. Quickly we discovered we did not have enough money to live on. The stress was overwhelming.

When we arrived in Honduras we found the team of Hondurans that we were to work with was not a team at all. After a year of working with a tutor and doing very little ministry, I was depressed. So I would have to "take care of myself" with masturbation, usually thinking about my wife, which made it somewhat ok, I thought.

Soon after cable came to our small town, I found myself occasionally watching a movie on TV late at night while everyone else was asleep. I even got caught by Suzanne once or twice watching something inappropriate. I would minimize it, confess to her, and be forgiven. I believed Suzanne accepted it because she thought, as many women think, that every man struggles with pornography. In reality it devastated her.

Finally, I had learned Spanish well enough to engage in ministry, but there was no team to work with, so I began ministering in our local church. It felt good and fulfilling. So masturbation and pornography diminished, but never went away completely. My dark secret could be contained for months at a time, and once for over a year. I found something that took away the feelings of shame. I could become someone that God liked and could even love over time, if I worked hard enough to gain His love. It was called ministry.

Several months later my good friend and ministry partner for the next six years, Jorge Espinal, asked if I wanted to go with him to train some pastors, and I said, "Yes!" We had such a great response to that conference that we were invited all over the country to teach our pastor conferences. It was awesome. It was a thrill, a rush, and something that I've only felt one other time in my life outside of drugs, masturbation, and pornography. It filled something empty in my heart, it seemed right, and it made me feel good.

As I look back, all I really did was substitute my shameful addictions for something else, without dealing with my core emotions. I changed from one thing that made me feel better to another thing I could do to feel better without the shame. I found something new to fill my void. It was ministry! I was getting a different type of fix through ministry and it was working.

I traveled relentlessly, leaving my wife at home with three small children. I felt that God was pleased with me, but it was deeper than that. Could God now love me? I worked even harder because I felt the need to balance out all my filthiness with good.

Don't get me wrong. This quest to be loved by God was not about salvation, even though I sometimes doubted my salvation. If I was truly a Christian would I continue to do the things that I was doing, such as masturbation and pornography? This new love I felt was an accepting type of love. God loves everyone. But now I felt He loved me because He was pleased I was doing so much for Him.

So, I continued to work harder. Jorge and I started a Mobile Bible Institute (MBI) that became very successful. We were intensely training seventy five pastors/church leaders in two different locations. We were getting requests from several other locations in Honduras to do the same. Other countries like El Salvador, Nicaragua and Panama asked us to start Mobile Bible Institutes in their countries as well.

God was definitely pleased with me now! I would talk about God's love, preach about God's love, but most of all I would work for God's love. I would go back to pornography when things were going wrong or in some kind of distorted celebration when others didn't want to celebrate. I would also masturbate when I felt like my wife wasn't taking care of my sexual needs. In my mind it was her fault.

On several occasions my wife threatened to leave and go back to the States to raise our children, because I was never home in Honduras. I would make her feel bad, ungodly, and unspiritual. I told her on several occasions if that was what she really wanted to do then that would be fine. I would say, "we'll pack up, go back to the states, and I will get a job, but only if you pray about it first." I would tell her I was sorry and that she had to forgive me, because that was the "spiritual" thing to do. I hurt my wife deeply over and over again. She requested that we get help, and I refused because of pride and fear of being found out. She felt uncared for, unappreciated, and abandoned. She was so far down on the list of my priorities. It is sad and embarrassing to me to this day. I don't know how nor why she stayed with me.

I was promoted to Latin American Director of my mission and we moved back to the USA. With this new position I was taking ten to twelve international trips a year helping other missionaries serve God. I was a pastor to missionaries. Because of my struggle, I set up personal boundaries, and ninety nine percent of the time I would honor them. I would not go into a newsstand in an airport because I knew there were magazines in the back corner. I would not leave an airport. I would stay around people.

I really loved my new ministry and I could go a good while without masturbating or needing pornography because I was helping so many people to do good things for God. He had to be pleased with me now!

Then the internet age came with unlimited access to the world of pornography. It was like finding the magazines under the bed for the first time all over again. What a rush! I would throw in the towel for days at a time, then hit my knees, on my face, and beg God to forgive me, and He would.

Almost every time I was sure that I had my breakthrough and I would never do it again. I would stay clean for months at a time but then fall back into it and have to confess all over again. I even asked God to expose me because I didn't have enough guts to tell anyone. I wanted freedom but I couldn't find it. So I worked even harder in ministry, trying in vain to balance out my sin with good deeds.

Many of you can identify with the cycle I was caught up in. I engaged in a lot of ministry with a little bit of masturbation and pornography. I was still ashamed, so I worked harder. I did more to balance out my dark secret. That went on for eighteen years! As I worked harder for God I needed masturbation and pornography less.

Finances were always tough as it is with most faith missionaries. I finally got a part time job, selling high-tech fire alarms. I felt better about myself because now I was providing for my family like never before. My family was able to have things that we never had before. We could even go out to eat on occasions. I was working at least sixty hours a week with the mission, and another twenty five with my new job. My wife was provided for and appreciated all my hard work. Things were going well.

Our relationship was closer than ever. I was successful in ministry and now in business. I was winning sales awards over men that were working full-time. I was winning trophies and exclusive trips through the business. I was able to take my family on vacations for the first time in my life, most of them provided by the business. Life was very good!

My wife was involved with two Bible studies and growing spiritually like never before. I was proud of Suzanne and I felt very close to her. The ministry was growing. I was recruiting Latin Americans to go to Europe, so my responsibilities grew. I was in charge of eighteen families in several countries around the world, not just in Latin America. I was traveling more, and when I was not traveling, I was working my part time job to continue to provide for my family. It seemed like I was winning the battle over my lustful addictions.

So what could go wrong? Everything!

I found out later that my wife, Suzanne, was praying at the time. Specifically, she was praying for the scales to be lifted from her eyes. She was also praying the prayer of Jabez, asking God to "bless us indeed and expand our borders of impact and ministry". God began to answer those prayers. It was not the answer that she was expecting, but God did answer her.

Chapter NINE

Finding Freedom the Hard way!

My Dark Secret Exposed

In May, 2004 I travelled to Albania to visit one of my Latin American missionaries. I felt strong and successful, so I broke a personal boundary. I had a nine hour layover in Amsterdam and I left the airport, thinking I was strong enough. I walked the streets of downtown Amsterdam for an hour, and turned the corner onto a road I had never seen before. It was a prostitute lane.

To my shame, a little later, I found myself in a room doing something I thought I would never do… being unfaithful to my wife with another woman, a prostitute. After about ten minutes, I burst out of that room in tears, talking out loud, and running through the streets of Amsterdam sweating profusely. I couldn't believe what I had done. I felt like people were moving away from me again like the parting of the Red Sea. I was as close as a man could get before going crazy. I was saying, "This is not me. I could not have done this. I didn't want to do this." My secret sin and fantasy life had caught up with me.

I made my way back to the airport bound train. The spiritual warfare in those moments was intense. NO ONE WOULD KNOW.... I DIDN'T DO THAT.... I CAN'T TELL ANYONE... MY WIFE WOULD KILL ME (NO SERIOUSLY, SHE SAID SHE WOULD KILL ME AND I BELIEVED IT).

The reality was that if I told anyone, I would lose my ministry, my wife, and my family. I cried out to God on that train, "I can't lose you, God". God gave me the strength and grace to make the decision to go home and tell my wife face to face. I changed my plane ticket to return to the States. Then I called my boss and my parents and confessed to them by phone from Amsterdam. I tried to resign from the mission but my boss would not accept it. He heard the pain in my voice. He was worried about me.

My parents were brokenhearted and deeply worried about me. I was not able to get a ticket all the way back to Birmingham. The General Director of our mission sent a coworker to meet me in New York, where I had a layover. I had been up over thirty hours with no sleep. When he picked me up at the airport he took me to a hotel and we talked for several hours. I got no sleep. I couldn't sleep because I couldn't believe what I had done. I was so ashamed.

Two days after leaving my home for Albania, I had to return to face my wife and tell her what I had done. She was not there, so I waited. She arrived about a half an hour later, but it seemed like a week. I'll never forget her face the moment she walked in the door. She saw immediately that something was wrong. She thought someone had died. She wanted to know who. She wanted me to just tell her.

I asked her to sit down but she could not. She pleaded, "Just tell me." I began to cry and couldn't get the words out. I was so ashamed. Finally I managed to speak the words I thought I would never have to say. "I have been unfaithful to you" (see Chapter 14 – Confession: How to Tell the Truth). She fell down to the floor and wept. She balled up in a fetal position and wept. Then she sat up and began hitting herself, hoping she was waking up from a bad dream. I wish it had been a dream.

After a long, gut-wrenching cry, she got up and demanded that our boss come to the house. He was there within a half an hour. She asked him how could this happen. She reminded him of a meeting she had with him a year earlier, in which she pleaded with him not to allow me to work so much. She was so angry at him. She was disappointed.

He encouraged her as best he could. He said, "We are going to get through this together." We talked and cried for over an hour. She asked how she was going to tell her family, because they needed to know. I did not think it would be fair for her to tell her family. So, I offered for us to go to her family, and I would confess to them the wrong that I've done to their daughter and to their sister.

So without any sleep we began the trip around Birmingham. We started with her parents. They were supportive and they forgave me. We went to each one of her sister's houses to confess to them as well. They too forgave me. One even offered help. Her husband told us they knew someone who could help us. We talked about a man named Eli. During that conversation, I felt that maybe, just maybe, we could make it through this.

About one week later, we were driving down the road and my wife received a phone call from a close friend. When Suzanne answered, her friend said; "I am so sorry for what has happened." Suzanne was unsure what her friend was talking about, so she asked. Her friend explained that she had received a letter from our mission. My wife burst into tears and slumped out of her seat into the floor board of our minivan. I pulled over and asked her what had happened. She said, "They know, everyone knows." I was not sure what she was talking about. She explained that her dear friend had received a letter from our mission. It said that I "had been caught" in a moral failure. I began to weep.

From the road side I called my pastor, Harry Walls, and choking through tears told him what we had just learned. He and his wife immediately got into their car to come meet us. I couldn't drive because I was crying so hard. He drove us to his house and ministered to us the rest of the afternoon. Suzanne sat on the porch swing with my pastor and he encouraged her. I saw her pain again and I was devastated. I feared that she would leave with our children, and I would be alone. I felt sick to my stomach. I walked off the porch and went to the Pastor's beautiful flower garden and began to dry heave. I couldn't bear this anymore. I didn't think our marriage would survive. More than half the people in our church had received that letter. It was humiliating and so embarrassing. The people I love were being hurt again because of me.

Six weeks later we finally met Eli Machen, the counselor my brother-in-law recommended, and started intensive counseling. We went away to Boone, North Carolina separately to attend a marriage workshop. I went for three days, and then Suzanne followed for three days. The purpose was to encourage us to focus on ourselves and what we needed to do to change, to improve ourselves, and to strengthen our marriage.

During that three day workshop my life was changed. Eli gave us homework the first night, but before we ended our session he encouraged us with James 5:16, which says to, *"confess your sins to one another and pray for one another so that you may be healed"*. Eli also said that this was a safe place, a place of restoration. It was a place that Galatians 6:1-3 would be applied:

> *"Brethren, even if anyone is **caught in any trespass**, you who are spiritual, **restore such a one in a spirit of gentleness**; each one looking to yourself, so that you too will not be tempted. Bear one another's burdens, and thereby fulfill the law of Christ. For if anyone thinks he is something when he is nothing, he deceives himself."*

I wanted to be restored. I wanted this healing. So with a lot of fear I did the homework. The next morning, for the first time in my life, I told a group of men my dark secret... all of my dark secret! To my surprise, I was accepted for who I was, not for what I could do. I was loved for being me, not for what I was doing for anyone. I was not judged or condemned, but understood in a way I have never been before. I also understood myself like never before. I was not ashamed, nor was I alone. I confessed all of my sins to this group of men and I felt something I had never felt.... a process of genuine healing had begun.

I had always confessed my sins to God, repeatedly. When I confessed to God, I was cleansed (I John 1:9) but I had never felt the healing that I felt that day. The healing process began that day and I have never been the same. I began to believe the truth of II Corinthians 4:2 "we (I) have renounced **the things hidden because of shame**, not walking in craftiness or adulterating the word of God, but by the **manifestation of truth** ....". I was set free from the lie of my dark secret that I had carried most of my life.

After that workshop, I came to realize that my biggest addiction over the past eighteen years was ministry. My definition of an addiction is anything someone runs to instead of God to fill a void in their life. That is what I was doing with ministry. So two months later, after meeting with my pastor several times, I resigned from the mission. It was one of the hardest decisions of my life, but one of the best. Since then, I have felt God's unconditional love for me, not based on what I can do for Him, but simply because He is God, I am His child and loves me regardless.

Life was not perfect over the next several years. Actually it was very difficult. I had two businesses that failed, taking us into bankruptcy, and we lost our home. I felt like I was in the desert many times, not knowing God's purpose of my life. Through those dark times God was faithful. He restored me with a purpose, and I am allowing God to use the dark secret of my past to help others find freedom.

Conclusion of PART TWO

Thank you for reading my story. As a reminder, I have not intended to offend anyone, but to offer hope and encouragement. I desired for you to feel what I felt at the time. Also, I hope that you were able to see how the same feelings seemed to build on each other, leading me to conclusions which were not all correct. Many of them defied God's word and what he says about Himself, me, and others. But at the time I thought they were correct, and that affected the way that I looked at important life situations, and how I saw people in my life.

While you were reading, I also hope you were able to see how faulty thinking can develop towards yourself, others, and God. They become *core beliefs*. I have experienced, and now teach, that to find freedom one must discover those core beliefs and understand that many core beliefs are really *unbelief* because they deny the mindset of God. The discovery of those core beliefs is the beginning of recovery, and recovery is a lifetime event until we see God face to face.

It is time to be honest about what is truly going on in our churches today. Again, my desire is neither to offend nor to excuse what I did, but to look at the facts. We cannot ignore the facts of pornography use:

➤ An internet survey conducted by Rick Warren of Saddleback Church in 2002 found 30 percent of 6,000 pastors had viewed internet porn in the last 30 days.

➤ In his book, "Men's Secret Wars", Patrick Means reveals a confidential survey of evangelical pastors and church lay leaders. Sixty-four percent of these Christian leaders confirm that they are struggling with sexual addiction or sexual compulsion including, but not limited to use of pornography, compulsive masturbation, or other secret sexual activity.

I give those stats because that is where I was, in leadership. If it is true of our leadership how much more is it true in the pews? This is not only a "man's struggle":

➤ 34% of readers of *Today's Christian Woman's* online newsletter admitted to intentionally accessing internet porn.

If you have a dark secret of sexual addiction, or feel you are living a lie, you can be free. If you need help, please contact me. You do not have to live in shame, you do not have to feel alone, and you can find freedom as I have.

At the writing of this book (2015), I have been free from masturbation, the use of pornography, and wrong motive for doing ministry for over eleven years. I must be honest. If someone had said eleven years ago that I would be able to make that claim, I would have said "Maybe others but not me, because I have tried!" The key is that I had tried by myself, and this, as with any addiction, is not a battle you can win alone. It is not easy. I had many tough moments, shed many tears, and without that group of men, especially my dear friend, Wade Hooper, standing with me, I would have failed again.

May you find hope through my story for you and for your spouse. May you find courage to reach out and find help to free yourself of the shame that controls you. Live in the light and be free from the power of keeping things in the dark.

PART THREE

Restoration of a Ministry to Broken Hearts

by Paul and Suzanne Talley

Introduction

As you read our stories it was obvious that God has had His hand on us even in the worst of times. We would have preferred God answer Suzanne's prayers in a different way, but we are glad that He answered them. Eli told us, early in recovery process, that one day we would look back and be able to thank God for all of this.

Today, we can both say that we are very thankful. That is not to say we are happy with the bad decisions we both made. But we can say we are overjoyed that God has taken those bad decisions and transformed our lives for His glory. He has changed us individually, and as a couple, and has used us to transform dozens of marriages.

Paul is glad he can say that he has been sober from his sexual and ministry addictions since 2004. He can also say that all the embarrassment, shame, and financial pain was worth it to experience the freedom, inward peace, and serenity that he feels today. He has loved getting to know himself, his needs, and his feelings. He likes himself and does not feel alone or awkward all the time, but accepted by others and by God without doing anything for them. He loves to do ministry without the burden of obligation, neither to fix others problem nor to receive God's love. Suzanne is pleased and can testify that she is living with a new man that strives to put her first above all things in this world while seeking God's direction for our lives.

Suzanne can honestly say that she is glad that she has been freed from the bondage of rage. She can also say that she is learning to release things (husband, kids, and ministry) into the hands of a loving God who cares for her and loves her without anything in return. Paul is pleased and can testify that he is living with a new woman that walks to the heartbeat of our God.

Our coupleship has been redefined and continues to be redefined to what true intimacy is supposed to look like. We have experienced and continue to experience a greater connection of safety and inward peace, but even more importantly, intimacy each day. We have learned to walk as "one flesh", having victory in our independence from each other, while at the same time depending on our loving God to work in our hearts as individuals and as a couple.

We have learned and try to live in the reality that we are not enemies but allies in this battle of marriage. We acknowledge that there is an enemy that is daily trying to destroy us individually, as a couple, and the ministry of CMIC. We have learned that we must walk in community (the body of Christ operating as a body of Christ) for these truths to continue to be true in our coupleship.

We live by and base our ministry on the fact that living in community is Biblical, honoring to God, and the only way to live in true joy and inward peace. Paul once received an email with a link to a video by author and speaker Paul Tripp from a friend that has walked with Paul for several years. He asked Paul to listen to the video, as it sounded like he and Paul Tripp were saying the same thing. We stay very busy, so when Paul pulled up this video on YouTube and saw that is was over fifty minutes long, he was hesitant. Several days later, Paul began to play it in the background while he was doing administrative work. He found himself stopping what he was doing and just listening, and then at 43:12 into this fifty minute video he heard Paul Tripp say the following:

> *"...here is what the call is; the call is for you and me to humbly and willingly live in intentionally intrusive, Christ-centered, grace driven, redemptive community. The "Jesus and me" religion of western culture is a delusion; it doesn't exist in the New Testament. You have been welcomed to a community of faith. You are in desperate need of those intentionally intrusive, Christ-centered, grace driven, redemptive moments... if you don't, you may be a Christian, but you are not living biblical Christianity because you cannot do this by yourself."*
>
> - Paul Tripp,
> *"Self-Examination Is a Community Project"*

Hebrews 3:13 says:

> *"But **encourage one another day after day**, as long as it is still called "Today," <u>so that</u> **none of you will be hardened by the deceitfulness of sin**."*

If you do not have this type of community in your life and marriage you are in danger of being *"hardened by the deceitfulness of sin."* Our desire is for each couple that enters the CMIC ministry to be placed in this type of community, and we pray that each of you will be able to find that type of community.

Part Three will allow you to see clearly how God has taken what Satan intended for our destruction and harm and turned it into something that is for our good and that glorifies Himself. We also will give some practical tools interwoven throughout the story of CMIC. As you read, we ask you to join us in praising Him for the great things He has done in us and through us!

Chapter TEN

The Key to our Healthy Marriage: The Check-in

The Long Journey to Start CMIC

In 2006, Paul left his full commission job because the economy took a huge hit and our sales were no longer enough for us to live on. When he left that job Suzanne asked him to consider going into full time ministry helping couples in crisis, as we were once in crisis. Paul was shocked by the suggestion. He said "no way" because he was afraid that he could not do ministry in a healthy way.

Paul will also admit today that it was because he does not like change. To him change was bad because it made him feel awkward and alone, like he felt so much growing up. He wanted us to simply continue as lay people helping troubled marriages. So Suzanne waited and prayed. Paul began to work as a handy man and it was amazing the way God kept bringing work and supplying for our needs.

After about eighteen months of doing handy man work an opportunity to buy a construction company came along. We went to our pastor, Harry Walls, for advice. He did not feel good about the opportunity, and during that conversation suggested that we should consider going into full time ministry helping couples in crisis. Suzanne looked at Paul and smiled. Again, Paul insisted that he was not ready, and probably never would be. He explained to our pastor that the construction opportunity would allow him to make a good living, which he had never consistently been able to do in twenty years of marriage. He wanted to give financially to the church and other ministries, and that excited Paul. So Suzanne waited and prayed.

Paul made the decision to buy the construction company. During that year the business lifted much of the financial strain we had been under since starting recovery, and really all our married life. We became givers and it was fulfilling to be able to help those in need. Paul would travel up to two weeks at a time out of town. This was not the ideal, but because we had learned some healthy tools for communicating, we made it work.

We would *check-in* with each other by phone throughout the day. This helped us stay connected. Sometimes we felt even more connected when he was on the road then when he was in town. Our check-ins became a crucial part of our recovery, and the biggest contributing factor to saving our marriage and developing true intimacy.

Eli taught us how to properly check-in with each other. He emphasized that we needed to develop a "show up" place. The show up place is a place of safety for us both. It is a place where we can be honest and vulnerable with each other. He also taught us that the foundation of showing up was with the check-in.

So let us explain what the check-in is so that it may help you. We learned many tools as we started recovery, but this one has been the most beneficial in saving our marriage, and is also the foundation of our ministry. If you don't do anything else we suggest, please do this. We have practiced this almost every day since 2004. If for some reason we miss a check-in we find ourselves assigning feelings to one another and begin to feel distant. We do not know the origin of the check in, but we have to give credit to Eli, who taught us this exercise. We have tweaked it some, but the fundamentals are the same.

This practical tool we use in communication is a fast but profound way to communicate on a heart level.

The *Check-in* is Two Questions and One Statement:
1. What is your <u>feeling word</u>?
2. What is your <u>need</u>?
3. I <u>affirm you</u> for (because) …..

Let us explain how it is done. First you ask if your spouse wants to do a *check-in*. They have the right to say yes or no. If they say "no", the one who initiated must respect their spouse's wishes not to engage at that moment. Out of respect the spouse who declined should advise when they will be willing to check-in at a later time. *Not checking-in should not be an option*. As a couple, you must be committed to connecting on at least a basic level every day.

If the response is "yes" then continue with the first question. If the answer is "no", the initiator will have the tendency to be offended, especially if they are struggling with co-dependency. That is a good time for the initiator to reach out to a trusted and safe friend.

Once the check-in is started and the spouse gives their feeling word, he or she then asks the initiator the same question: "What is your feeling word?" The initiator must wait until they are asked what their feeling word is to insure they are not controlling their spouse and that the spouse is engaging.

The feeling word is one word with no explanation before or after. It is a feeling not a thought. It is you evaluating at that moment where you are emotionally. You should take into consideration all the things that are going on in your world at that time. For example: Have the kids been driving you up the wall? Are you stressed with work? Did you make a big sale today? Did you get all the clothes washed? Take it all in and give one word with no explanation!

The initiator after stating their feeling word then goes to the second question. Your need could be a need from God, emotional need, spiritual need, personal need that only you can meet, or a need you are requesting of your spouse. This need <u>is not just one word</u> but should be stated in one or two sentences and <u>not in a paragraph</u>. It should be very clear, concise and to the point. The need should not be used in a manipulative way to get your spouse to do something they don't want to do. It should not be presented as a command but as a request.

Your spouse, as always, has the right not to meet that need. If it is a healthy request, do everything possible to meet that need with the goal of expressing your love or respect to your spouse. If you don't think you can meet that need don't say so at this time, but wait until the check-in is over. This will keep you from having an argument in the middle of the check-in and risk not finishing it. Sometimes a little explanation or clarification is needed, but not during the actual check-in. <u>Any explanation or clarification should be done after your check-in is complete</u>.

Finally, the initiator makes their statement of affirmation to their spouse. The spouse should recognize or receive the affirmation verbally with a "thank you" or "I appreciate that". Then the invited spouse gives their statement of affirmation to the initiator. The spouse's affirmation should be recognized as well with a "thank you" or "I appreciate that".

This completes the check-in. Then it is time to ask questions or seek clarification, if needed, but we suggest that does not happen often. We say that for many reasons but most importantly is the fact that it will prolong the check-in. If every time it is prolonged then what we have found is that the couple will not do it as often. But if you guard that five minutes time frame then it will happen more often and more consistent. Also, for the sake of safety, being real without fear, or breaking co-dependency, the spouse can say "no" to any discussion or clarification. But both parties must recognize if one or both says "no" that hurt or disappointment might result, especially on the need portion.

You may be thinking, "Why is the check-in so methodical?" If there is no discussion during the actual "check-in" it should take only five minutes. Sometimes it could be longer if it takes a while to know your feeling word or need. For Paul, that was very hard at the beginning, because he lived so long denying that he had feelings or needs.

Keeping it short is important. We have found that when there is no communication, it is often because a spouse does not want to engage, or does not have time to engage in a long conversation. Keeping it short will allow more frequency and as a result deeper intimacy. After regular use of the check-in we have seen conversations develop in couples that never had conversations. We have also seen long conversations will go deeper because each spouse feels safe with the other.

We have had some couples resist doing check-ins, as Paul did in the beginning, because it seems so childish or so awkward. If you give it a try we believe you will never regret it.

Here is a brief list of what the check-in will do for you as a couple:

1. The couple with good communication will improve even more.

2. A couple that is struggling with communication will have a method to develop it in a simple, safe, and practical way.

3. For those who are really busy the check-in gives them a way to connect without fear or concern about having time for a long conversation.

4. It helps those who struggle with expressing their feelings to open up and eventually come alive and enjoy sharing their heart.

5. The check-in gives the co-dependent a starting point to break the destructive cycle of co-dependency on many different levels. One example would be, not allowing your feeling word or need to be affected by your spouse. A second would be allowing your spouse to feel the way they feel without trying to change them.

6. For the spouse that doesn't feel pursued it allows their spouse an opportunity to pursue without pressure.
7. For the spouse who feels controlled it gives them an opportunity to comfortably connect with their spouse.

8. For the spouse who feels smothered it allows them to be able to connect in a non-threatening way.

If you both commit to regular check-ins your relationship will grow in ways you cannot even imagine. We firmly believe that in the beginning the husband should take the lead to get to *the show-up place* and initiate the check-in. We say that because we have seen so many relationships driven emotionally and spiritually by the wife, which keeps the man from doing what God has called him to do - to be the leader. As time goes by and regular check-ins take place, then the wife can begin to initiate as well. When that occurs, it is very satisfying to both husband and wife, as each feels pursued by the other, a core need that we all have.

Chapter ELEVEN

An Umbrella Counseling Firm to Formation of CMIC

How CMIC Came Into Being

Several of the couples we had been helping, while Paul was still running his business, went from being in crisis to having solid marriages. They were so grateful to find their healing and they began to ask us; "Why don't you do this full time?" Paul would always answer that question the same as before and Suzanne would wait and pray. We refused to be paid for our help. We would say that this was not our job and we were simply paying forward what we had received.

After about a year of the construction job, things went south with the company's owner and Paul was losing the opportunity to buy it. Crisis had returned. Do we fight this or do we let it go?

We went again to seek council from our pastor. After he had heard what was happening with the buying of the company he looked at Paul with a smile and asked, "Are you ready now?" Suzanne finally spoke up and explained that she had been praying and has felt that it was time for us to return back to ministry for several years. She also told him that some of the couples we had been helping had been asking "Why aren't you doing this full time?" She continued by saying, "and now you, our pastor, are suggesting the same thing!"

Suzanne finished speaking to our pastor and turned and looked at Paul, smiling. So with butterflies in his stomach, Paul decided that God must truly be speaking. He would be willing to explore it but only if we had people around us that would advise us and support us so that Paul would not do ministry again with the wrong motive. Everyone agreed.

Our pastor also encouraged us to go and talk to a Christian Counseling Firm that we had developed a relationship with while we were building a lay counseling ministry at our church. The Executive Director of this firm liked what we were doing with the lay counseling ministry. So we left our pastor's office and asked to talk to him. He listened and then got very excited and started to dream with us. We were hired on the spot under their non-profit umbrella.

So that day we walked away from a potential six figure job to zero, as we had to raise our support to be able to live! Paul wondered if we were crazy. As we look back even today, we scratch our heads and think, "Were we crazy?"

We put together an advisory board of trusted people that knew our story, especially Paul's eighteen year affair with the *mistress of ministry*. We firmly believed that this board should be made up of couples, and not the typical board of mostly men. Our financial situation got intense but God never let us down. We saw Him do incredible things. We have many "loaves and fish" stories to tell. He has truly blessed us over these years.

We thank God for providing that umbrella and safety of that firm. During the next two years we saw our ministry explode. We went from working with one or two couples at a time to quickly having eight couples in less than two months. We developed *Couple Recovery Groups* and had great success. As soon as we would place one more couple into a group they were replaced by two more new couples needing help. It started to get out of control, so our advisory board decided to hold us accountable for how many couples we could see in a day and how many couples we could see in a week. Everyone was excited to see what God was doing through us and this ministry.

Paul applied and got accepted into the IITAP (International Institute for Trauma and Addiction Professionals) program formed by Dr. Patrick Carnes, the pioneer of sex addiction treatment. It was such an honor. After two plus years of intense study where Paul learned about the cutting edge 30 Task Model developed by Patrick Carnes, he became a Pastoral Sexual Addiction Professional (PSAP). It was a leap of faith, because it was an expensive program, but God provided.

The knowledge Paul gained through this education has been priceless. The research and resources available to us as a result of being a PSAP are endless. Now Paul has access to assessment tools through IITAP that allow us to have a better understanding of the couple's sexual issues, post-traumatic issues, and money issues. These assessment tools help us decide whether to refer out or work with the couple.

As we continued to grow, at one point having thirty nine couples in some stage of crisis, we developed a couples' workshop to provide help in a more intense and structured way. This was quite successful. Suzanne wanted us to develop an individual workshop as well, but Paul thought it was better to send them away for individual workshops with another ministry.

This other ministry, as well as the counseling firm we were under, began to feel a little uncomfortable with the way we were doing ministry. They felt what we were doing was too far outside of the "norm" of how counseling was done. We struggled through that and continued to help change marriages.

We never had an office at the firm, but rather at our church, which raised questions about what we were actually doing. When we met with the Executive Director or for lunch with the counseling group of the firm, they were overwhelmed by all we were involved with. We believed in the principle of walking with couples, not only counseling them. It was intense. But we firmly believe that couples in crisis need that kind of intensity, as we did. We also believe on a personal level that if we had gone to the typical counselor and done the typical counseling we would have not made it. For example, we do two hours sessions not just one hour. Our clients were allowed to call us at any hour of the night to talk through their struggles. We were not charging for our services. Lives were being changed and marriages were being saved! God was blessing!

We were asked by the Executive Director of the firm to develop an outreach program for the local churches. So we did. The goal was to help couples in the church before they had a crisis. We eventually developed a church workshop that is called **Understanding Eden**. It is based on the fact that we cannot truly understand the dynamics in a marriage nor understand the commands found in Ephesians 5 or I Peter 3 about marriage until we understand what happened in the Garden of Eden. It has been impactful to the churches that have received it. If you want more information on that workshop please visit our website:

www.christianmarriagesincrisis.com.

In 2011, we decided to host a golf tournament to raise funds for our counseling ministry. We worked a lot of crazy hours but still struggled to make ends meet financially. The golf tournament helped financially, but it also gave us more exposure, and as a result more work. Our advisory board looked at our continued financial struggle and asked what could be done. They knew that the counseling firm was removing an administrative fee for their services and questioned if we should continue or go independent. In the beginning it was for credibility, but over time our results truly gave us credibility. All of our referrals were by couples that had gone through our ministry, or by someone associated with our ministry. They were not coming from the counseling firm, which was the plan from the beginning.

Our advisory board challenged us to consider removing ourselves from the counseling firm to become an independent ministry. That scared us, mainly Paul, so we waited. We continued to grow as a ministry and develop materials. We also talked to the elders of our church about what was being suggested. Everyone was in agreement that this was the direction we should go. Finally, after almost a year of talking about it with our advisory board, the elders and our pastor, on March 1, 2012 we filed in Shelby County of the state of Alabama a Certificate of Formation of a non-profit organization called *Christian Marriages in Crisis* (CMIC). Our advisory board officially became a Board of Directors of CMIC.

The transition from the counseling firm to CMIC went smoothly, and we were thankful. We continued to grow and Paul finally saw the need to develop an individual recovery workshops for men and women. The changes we saw as a result of the individual workshops only improved what we were trying to do through our ministry.

The Individual Workshops (IW) we do are called *Intensives* by other counselors and organizations. This is because of the amount of work that is done, the depth of the work that is done, and the short amount of time that it is done in. We were told before going to our first IW that it was the equivalent to about six to twelve months of individual counseling. We experienced that in our own journey and have seen it in others.

Our IW begins on a Friday night at 6 p.m. and goes through Sunday at noon. By design the spouse is away for two nights and we ask them to "unplug" from their world. Unlike our IW in which Paul went first, we decided that it was best for the wives to go first, and then the following weekend the husbands. Those days in between the two weekends can be very interesting.

Often a couple is ready to seek out help only after a major crisis, as in our case. It can be difficult to convince the "non-offending" spouse to see the need of going to a workshop. We are aware that occasionally the non-offending spouse only goes so that their spouse who has offended or hurt them deeply will go. We are okay with that because we know they will discover much about themselves if they attend. Getting them both to an IW is important because the "presenting problem" i.e. unfaithfulness, an affair, pornography, or rage is not the real problem; it is so much deeper than that. When we feel hesitancy by the non-offending spouse we encourage them to attend so that they can find healing for themselves even if the relationship doesn't survive. We emphasize their need of healing so that they will not bring hurt or pain into another relationship.

 The separation of the husband and wife for the IW's is important so that we can focus on getting to know each spouse. This also allows the husband or wife to look inward instead of pointing fingers outwardly. In all marriages, we have the tendency to point the finger at the other and blame or correct each other. Our goal in doing the IW's is to allow each person to step back, look at themselves, and own what they need to change. In any conflict, great or small, both spouses could have done things differently or better, but sometimes it is hard to see. But when a marriage is in a crisis, no matter how bad the situation, both spouses need to identify what they could have done better. The IW allows that to take place.

Intensive teaching on Friday night sets the foundation for the weekend. We talk about the chaos that is involved with change. In doing that, we try to get them to embrace the chaos presently and in the future so that change can happen. By using the Iceberg Reality by Virginia Satir, we show them that we want to go deep below the surface to their core "unbelief's" they have about themselves, others (including their spouse), and God.

We call those unbelief's *strongholds*, or the lies they believe. This is important because until they see the lies and connect the dots, no real change can happen. We end up the evening by talking about the power of our words, first to others, but then to themselves, by looking at James 4 and several others scriptures. When we are finished we give them homework designed to help them go down to the core beliefs that have shaped them and the way they operate relationally.

Saturday morning is spent helping individuals identify the unhealthy cycle(s) they are in and explaining how they can stop by establishing healthy habits. Intercessory prayers are made for the attendees throughout the afternoon, and it is powerful. Saturday is a day when the process of individual healing truly begins. They are given more homework for Saturday night. This time we are asking them to develop a new vision, as we did with Eli in our IW's. Based on *"Where there is no vision, the people are unrestrained, But happy is he who keeps the law"* Proverbs 29:18 (NASB)

Sunday morning consists of more teaching, but in a very interactive way, and it helps bring it all together. We end the morning and workshop with each attendee sharing their new vision for their lives. The workshop closes again with prayer for each attendee, that God would help them to fulfill their new vision, which we call working their individual recovery. Everyone is exhausted but fulfilled.

After being active in a *Couples Recovery Community*, which we will talk about in the next chapter, for several months they attend another workshop called the Couples Workshop (CW). This workshop is very intensive but much more interactive. As a result we need more time, so we start Friday morning and go through Sunday afternoon. In this workshop we begin by reminding them what they learned in the IW. During the Friday morning session we talk about the difference between individual recovery and couples recovery. Once that is understood we begin to teach various communication skills.

Friday afternoon we do things to open their eyes to their unhealthiness as a couple. All afternoon, we talk about the couple's idea of a Biblical marriage, what in reality their marriage looks like, and what healthy marriages should look like. Most couples point back to this time as pivotal in changing *their dance* of as a couple

Friday evening they have a homework assignment working on how to communicate properly. Many couples, as we did, get into a fight while doing this homework. We help them on Saturday morning to push through their disagreements. When they are finished the couple is in a better place to communicate in the future. It enables them to have disagreements rather than fights as they had in the past.

Saturday morning we talk about Understanding Negative Emotions. Suzanne is vulnerable with her recovery in this area, explaining how it affected her, Paul, and others that she loves and cares for. Paul explains how he enabled her by trying to "help" but discovered how it was pushing her deeper into her rage. It is a very eye opening time for many of the couples as they tend to struggle in this area.

Saturday after lunch while everyone is fresh we dive into what biblical healthy sexuality is and what it is not. Many of these couples are uncomfortable with this subject, so we try to be truthful and sensitive at the same time. The rest of the afternoon we use interactive teaching methods that help each spouse to discover the messages they live by and how they are damaging themselves, as well as their spouse. That night we ask them to develop a Couples Shield so that they have a vision as a couple, just as they have individually.

Sunday morning we try to bring it all together by doing an exercise in which they play out the drama that is typically going on in their marriage. It is amazing what happens that morning, how the lights come on, and the understanding that is gained through this exercise. We end the morning and workshop with each couple sharing their shield and being prayed over, asking God to allow their vision to be realized.

At the writing of this book, we have seen over 100 couples since 2010. During this time some of those couples quit after discovering the hard work that was necessary to heal their marriage and we have lost contact. But out of all the couples that have gone through the CMIC program, we have had only 3 couples decide to not continue their marriage. God has used the ministry to save dozens of marriages and now some of them are helping others as well for which we *Praise the Lord*!

Chapter TWELVE

Couple to Couple Counseling to CMIC Recovery Groups!

The Growth and Maturation of CMIC

You might wonder how it is possible for Paul and Suzanne to work with so many couples at the same time in this intensity. The answer is we cannot. As we mentioned in the last chapter we have developed Couple Recovery Groups or Communities. In my final PSAP training module Dr. Patrick Carnes talked about his philosophy regarding the most effective therapeutic approach. He suggested using a layered effect including individual therapy for both partners, family therapy, Twelve Step meetings for both partners, and finally, couple's therapy sessions and couple's support groups (including fellowships). We couldn't agree more.

Paul remembers sitting in the first PSAP training module where individual recovery was strongly emphasized to the point he thought, "Why am I sitting here? I am out of place!" But after each module unfolded, he could see how important the information was and how he could use it in helping the couples that God sent us. For us, hearing a man that is so respected in the addiction world note the importance of Twelve Step fellowships like Recovering Couples Anonymous (RCA) and Couple Recovery Groups was very refreshing. We have moved from calling them groups to calling them communities because we believe that is more accurate to what God has called us to do as the body of Christ.

We have had as many as four Couple's Recovery Communities spread throughout the Birmingham metro area and three couples Skyping into them from other States. When we had four we only had to facilitate two and the other two we oversaw. We are able to do that because we have strong leaders, experienced in recovery, leading them. We would visit those two communities every four to six weeks, but we are in communication each day through a medium of the *GroupMe* app on our phones.

Let us explain the healing process that we have developed. A person contacts us by phone, email, website, or text requesting help. We ask some basic questions about them to see if we need to refer them to someone else. Once we believe we can help, we tell them their spouse must contact our spouse, so that we can make sure they both want help. We will only help couples that both feel they need our help. Once that is established, we set up an appointment time.

At their first appointment, after a brief introduction, we take about forty five minutes to tell this new couple our story, as you have already read, but not as in-depth. When we started this ministry we developed a vision statement that we still hold to today, *Finding Hope...Redefining Intimacy*. When we finish our story we tell them that there are two reasons for sharing it. First, we want to give them hope by seeing that if God can take all our MESS and make it a MESSage, He can do the same for them. Second, we want them to know that the couple sitting in front of them will not sit in judgment of them. We have found that the vulnerability of telling our story first releases them to go into a deeper explanation of why they have come to see us. They feel a safety that they have never felt, and they don't feel alone in their struggle anymore.

After that we ask, "Why are you here and how we can help?" It is amazing what we learn the next hour as we hear their story. When they both finish telling their story and telling us how they think they need help, we thank them. We do not to allow them to set up their next appointment at that time. Instead we give them a packet. This packet explains that CMIC is a non-profit organization and we do not charge for our services, but would like them to give back to the ministry. It also includes personal data sheets that ask personal questions about medical, spiritual, and emotional conditions. They each have received a packet and we tell them that the personal information will not be shared until needed, and when all are in agreement. The last item in the packet is a contract. We ask them to read over it and sign it. It explains what we are going to require of them. We have found this to be valuable for them and for us, because they actually know what is expected of them.

We tell them to take home their packet and look it over. If they are both in agreement then they can set up their second appointment. We plan out the next several appointments. We place them with encouragers - people that have been involved in the ministry for a while that have similar stories of their own. In this way they do not feel alone. This also takes away some of the burden from us until they can get into a community. We will look at the dates of our next Individual Workshops and make sure they are available to attend. The IW is part of their contract.

Once they have attended their Individual Workshops, we will get together to debrief and talk about placing them into a Couples Recovery Community. When we place new couples into a community we discuss the purpose at that meeting so that the new couple(s) will know and the old couples will be reminded. This allows everyone to be with one mind.

We would like to share what we read to the community so that it may help you evaluate the group you are involved in, or help you develop a community that will be healthy for you and others who attend. This is what we read through and agree to as a community:

Gospel Centered Couples Recovery Community

Why are we moving you from Couple Accountability to a Couples Recovery Community for Accountability?

We believe that the group dynamic, where people learn from each other as well as from the facilitator(s), has been shown by research to be more effective than individual or couple counseling both in terms of initial results and long-term recovery. Most people report the healing they find in group accountability is more powerful than anything they have ever experienced. All of this research is mostly secular based but is what we have experienced as well. Through all our training we have heard this but then usually hear; "and we are not sure why but it works." We know why it works, even in a secular group, like AA, NA, or SA. It works because it is Biblical. It is what the Bible has called the church to do. It is what some refer to as "body life" that the church should be living but in a lot of situations it is not.

This is the way we see it:

Accountability	Result	Reason
No Accountability	**Isolation and Death**	Unbiblical
Individual Accountability	**Can hide sin & develop walls in coupleship**	Good
Couples Counseling	**Harder to hide sin & builds your coupleship**	Better
Couples Community	**Builds coupleship in Community – The Body**	Best

What we feel a Couples Recovery Community is _NOT_:

What do we see as some _Problems_ with the typical "accountability groups":

❖ Most accountability groups only address the sin and/or the behavioral component.

❖ Most accountability groups are only about reporting failures.

❖ Most Christian accountability groups' solution to failure or "acting out" is more prayer, Bible study or "try harder!"

Why do we feel the typical accountability group have these problems?

There are known _"Dysfunctional Family Rules"_ and we believe they are the same in typical church rules and as a result they over flow into church accountability groups:

1. **Don't _TALK_**

     • If we express a doubt in our faith, Scripture or love for our spouse...we hear... "Oh, brother (sister) don't talk that way!", "Just trust God, it will all work out."

- **Translation:** "I don't want to hear it and you are not allowed to voice those kinds of thoughts."

2. **Don't *FEEL***

   - We are allowed to feel happy, obedient ("have faith") or be positive *BUT* not to feel sad, afraid or angry.

   - **Translation:** "I don't want to hear what you feel and you are not allowed to feel or your feelings are wrong!"

3. **Don't *TRUST***

   - Things shared in private...make it back as a prayer requests or gossip.

   - Things shared in weakness...will backfire, disqualifies you or only encourages a condemning rebuke.

   - **Translation:** "I can't open up, people can't keep their mouth shut, and if you share, I can tell others if it is for your best...for prayer!"

What do we feel a "true accountability group" *IS.* It is a community:

❖ Accountability is place of **complete safety**. *This is and will be our first priority*.

"what is said here stays here"
"who comes here and why they come here stays here"

We are not to tell others that we are in a Couples Recovery Community together. We can say we are in a community and why we are in a community but we are NOT to ever name another person or couple in that conversation. In public the group facilitators (in this case us the Talley's) will act like we do not know you in public, for your protection and safety, because people know what we do. But feel free to acknowledge us, greet us, and introduce us at your discretion using your own description of who we are i.e. "old friends", "good friends" or "our group leader/ facilitators". We will always follow your lead.

❖ Accountability is a place of **FULL disclosure**. When there is full disclosure that is the foundation to *true safety*.

"Therefore confess your sins to each other and pray for each other so that you may be healed"
James 5:16

❖ Accountability should address the sin and/or the behavioral component **by trying to understand the heart or core issue of unbelief**.

> *"The heart is deceitful above all things and desperately wicked: who can know it"*
> **Jer. 17:9**

❖ Accountability should be a **development of true intimacy** by the first three functioning properly.

> *"Therefore be clear minded and self-controlled so that you can pray. Above all, love each other deeply, because love covers over a multitude of sins." **I Peter 4:7-8***

❖ Accountability should involve **successes**, no matter how small they might be.

> *"Encourage one another and build each other up"*
> **I Thess. 5:11**

❖ Accountability should involve what **longings/ triggers** you have discovered.

> *"…we ourselves GROAN within ourselves, waiting eagerly for our adoption as sons, the redemption of our body"* **- Romans 8:23**

❖ Accountability should involve **continued full disclosure** of recognized and/or newly recognized triggers and/or failures.

❖ Accountability **should not be about reporting failures but learning**:

   1. How *to reach out* before you fail
      ✓ First admit you have been triggered or admit feeling the "hole" or "groaning of the soul" i.e. emptiness or boredom.

   2. If you failed to reach out – **Confession**:
      ✓ First to God

      ✓ Second to your partners who you have offended and devalued.

      ✓ Then report your sin failure

❖ Accountability should be with the understanding that **Pornography, Masturbation, Binge/Over Eating, Drugs, over drinking, and etc are addictive types of behavior** and should not be minimized but addressed openly not as *THE* problem but a symptom of a deeper struggle.

❖ Accountability should be with the understanding that **no lasting change in addictive type of behavior will come without the help of others**.

"Brothers, if someone is caught in a sin, you who are spiritual should restore him gently" **Gal 6:1**

❖ Accountability should be in community because we need both *Accountability* and what we call *Support.* Accountability and Support are similar but not the same and we need both. One person or "sponsor" usually cannot consistently give both but a community typically can.

    1. **Accountability** – someone that will confront and even make you feel uncomfortable at times by speaking truth in love.

    2. **Support** – someone that will love and stand by you no matter what, even if you repeatedly sin, minimize, or deflect.

❖ Accountability should be with the understanding that *a lot* of people have as **their core beliefs:**

    1. I am basically a bad, unworthy person.

2. If you really knew me you wouldn't love/like me.

3. I can't depend on others to meet my needs - I have to meet them myself.

❖ Accountability should be with the understanding that there are **two types of purity**:

1. At Salvation - purity imparted to us by God.

2. With Sanctification - purity developed through walking out your obedience before God.

❖ Accountability should be with the understanding that **Jesus Christ death was for _TWO_ reasons**:

1. **Reconcile us to God** (Rom. 5:10; II Cor. 5:18-20; Col. 1:22)

"For if, when we were God's enemies, we were reconciled to him through the death of his Son, how much more, having been reconciled, shall we be saved through his life!" **Rom. 5:10**

2. **Reconcile us to one another**

"Therefore, if you are offering your gift at the altar and there remember that your brother has something against you; leave your gift there in front of the altar. First go and be reconciled to your brother; then come and offer your gift."

Matthew 5:23-24

What is our focus to be in a Gospel Centered Couples Recovery Community?

Let us look at an article written by *Jonathon Dodson* that we adapted for this community. He talks about our three fold purpose: *Identification, Mortification, and Sanctification*.

I. Identification: <u>Know your Sin</u>

Identify your personal patterns of sin and share your places of temptation with others you trust. For example:

> ➢ Does sexual lust creep in or your desire to crawl into bed and pull the covers over your head on Mondays after a demanding day of

144

ministry on Sunday or any day after a tough day of work?

➢ Are you tempted to view porn or go into your "rabbit hole" after a disagreement or frustration with your spouse?

➢ Does sexual temptation increase or anger develop after watching a movie with sexual humor or innuendo?

We would like to add to what *Jonathon Dodson* is saying here. When he says to share your specific patterns of temptation with someone you trust. We believe temptation is not a sin. If it were Christ would have been a sinner. But when you give in to your temptation it must be confessed. First, confess your sin to God (I John 1:9) for cleansing, and then to a trusted person (James 5:16) for healing.

We must bring things out of the darkness into the light. When things are left in the darkness (unconfessed) sin controls us, but when it is exposed (confessed) to the light we can control it. Confession breaks the power of private sin. By going public with our sin we heighten the tension between sin and holiness, fostering the mindset of mortification. Ask your trusted person to help you mortify (kill) sin by reminding you to avoid these patterns and places of unbelief. Identification or *knowing our sin* is the first principle for gospel accountability.

Now let us go back to what *Jonathon Dodson* is saying.

II. Mortification: <u>Be killing sin lest it be killing you</u>.

John Owen reminds us of our relentless foe when he writes: "Be killing sin lest it be killing you."

It is critical that we help one another fight the good fight of faith (1 Timothy 6:12; 2 Timothy 4:7). Mortification is the habitual weakening of sin through constant fighting and contending in the Spirit for victory over the flesh. We need the Spirit to fight, and we need to remind one another to rely on Him for mortification.

Gospel accountability doesn't just identify patterns; it asks questions. We should pay attention to the kind of questions we ask. Are we asking moralistic questions or gospel questions, questions that reinforce moral performance or questions that encourage faith in Christ? Our questions should be pointed and point to Christ. For example, instead of asking one another:

➤ "Did you view porn this week?"

➤ "Did you go into your rabbit hole this week?"

> "Did you masturbate this week?"

> "Did you play detective this week?"

Ask a question that points to sin and beyond to Christ.

> Are you finding your pleasure in Christ or in porn?

> Are you running from or to Christ?"

> Are you relieving your anxiety through faith in Jesus or through masturbation?"

> Are you trusting yourself or Christ to do the work in your spouse?"

Gospel accountability strengthens our resolve to cherish Christ over the fleeting promises of sin. It helps us put to death the lies of sin and trust the truth of the gospel. Mortification or *killing sin* is the second principle in gospel accountability.

III. Sanctification: <u>Set thy faith on His promises</u>.

We are always exercising faith…. trusting God or something else. We might put our faith in the promise of deep pleasure from viewing porn or if we pull the covers over our head things will get better. Or we might rely on knowing all, "playing detective", or in other words, controlling our spouse. Or turn to masturbation to relieve us from anxiety, frustration, or fear. These sins are acts of faith, albeit placed in unworthy and unreliable objects. Owen reminds us that we should set our faith on God's promises.

Very often we take God's promises for granted. We read them but don't believe them. Instead of trusting God's Word, we use it for a speech for our spouse, to point out how unbelieving our spouse is, or to build our case against our spouse. Other times, we pilfer through His promises for an experiential buzz for ourselves, but rarely do we look to trust Christ in His promises. Consider some of the following promises that point us to Christ:

➢ "Blessed are the pure in heart, for they shall see God." (Matthew 5:8)

➢ "Casting all your anxiety on Him, because He cares for you. Be of sober spirit, be on the alert..." (I Peter 5:7,8a)

➢ "Beloved, we are God's children now, and what we will be has not yet appeared; but we know that when he appears we shall be like him, because we shall see him as he is. And everyone who thus hopes in him purifies himself as he is pure." (1 John 3:2-3)

➢ Be anxious for nothing, but in everything by prayer and supplication with thanksgiving let your requests be made known to God. And the peace of God, which surpasses all comprehension, will guard your hearts and your minds in Christ Jesus. (Phil. 4:6-7)

> "Flee from youthful lusts and pursue righteousness, faith, love and peace along with those who call on the Lord from a pure heart." (2 Timothy 2:22)

Those who pursue purity will become pure at Christ's return. Those who pursue reliance on Christ can enjoy the hope of His coming. Those who cultivate a pure heart will see God. Those who pursue trusting Christ, their hearts and minds will be guarded by Him.

Our pursuit of purity and our pursuit of reliance on Christ should be done in community, with the help of others who are trusting in the Lord. Gospel accountability should compel us to treasure Christ over all other fleeting promises.

After reading this together as a community we open it up for questions and discussion. Community members usually express their feelings of being vulnerable and each issue is addressed.

The way we facilitate our CMIC Couples Recovery Communities is by starting with several questions to gage where everyone is and know how to proceed with the night.

Our first question is the same as the check-in that they are doing as a couple; "What is your feeling word?" We go around the room and each gives their feeling word without discussion.

We then ask; "On a scale of 1 to 10 what is their connection level (how close that they feel) to God?" After they all answer we ask the same of their coupleship connection, 1 to 10.

The last question we always ask is: "Do you need the group or are you here for the group, and on a scale of 1 to 10 what is your need to talk to the group?" We do that because we believe in the foundational principle that *we need the group or the group needs us.* To say that same thing in a Christian Community, as all our communities are, would be *"we need the Body of Christ or the Body of Christ needs us, because we are part of a body and we cannot do this alone."*

These questions are designed for two purposes; first to give couples the opportunity to be open and vulnerable, and second to know how as facilitators we need to proceed. Over the next hour and forty-five minutes all of us listen and learn. Our communities are different in that we allow "cross-talk." In the secular and even Christian recovery world that is discouraged because they believe that has the danger of trying to fix one another. But our belief is that we need one another because we all have the Spirit of God residing in us, and we all can help direct or give guidance, not fix one another. As everyone watches, listens, and gives feedback to the couples talking we can all learn as we see ourselves in many ways, either on an individual level or in the coupleship dynamic.

Depending on the size of the community not all couples get the time to talk but not all need to talk, as their talk number might be low. Even if their number is high, sometimes the couple can leave frustrated, as there was not enough time to deal with all the issues. It is a hard balance to keep but when more time is needed and the couple cannot wait to the next week, they can set up to meet with another couple outside of community time, or set up a session time with us.

Chapter THIRTEEN

Our Vision for CMIC
and
Some Key Thoughts

Our Vision for CMIC

As the ministry of CMIC has grown, we have seen that we cannot do this alone. As with any ministry a continual evaluation and revaluation of the ministry must be in place. In that process we have seen the need for help. As more and more couples have come to the ministry we have lost the ability to deal with *Individual Recovery* for each of these couples. Our desire is to bring on more couples to help the ministry with the influx of couples, but first to bring on a couple that can focus on the individual's struggles that each may have.

The Board of CMIC began to investigate what we would need to do to accomplish that. The first was to get office space. Up until now we have been partnering with four churches around the Birmingham metro area to house our counseling sessions and community meetings. In 2015, we took a leap of faith and secured our first office space.

The second was to find a couple with the same passion we have for marriages to be saved out of crisis, but with the desire to help the individuals. As a board we are trying to find that couple. At the writing of this book two couples have expressed interest but both decided later that they could not do the task at hand which has been a source of great discouragement but we have seen it as God protecting us and the ministry of CMIC.

Our complete vision for CMIC is to have a Recovery Center where hurting individuals and couples can come to for healing. Because our crisis began while we were in ministry we want this recovery center to have many facets. First, somewhere where pastors, missionaries, and full-time ministry workers can find safety to get the help they need, or a place to just get away for a few days. Second, because of our renewal of wedding vows in a beautiful garden was a crucial part of our recovery, especially Suzanne's, it is also a part of the vision for the future of CMIC. It will be a place to reveal God's peaceful rest through His attribute to reveal beauty through flower gardens and soothing sounds of water from a waterfront retreat center. We don't know where, how, or when it will happen, but we believe that God has given this vision to us through the prayer that Suzanne prayed many years ago.... before we entered into our crisis.

This would be a place with many cabins for couples to stay, as well as a conference center for meetings, workshops and conferences. It is a big dream and sometimes we lack the faith to believe it will come about, but we both feel in our hearts that it will. Our first workshops were in the mountains on the Tennessee and North Carolina boarder. It is a peaceful place, where you can take a walk in the woods and talk with God. A major part of Paul's recovery has been on the water while fishing, just riding in a boat, and sitting by a lake. So we envision those two aspects to be part of this location. To accomplish that, we would need a lot of woodsy land with a small to large lake. We would need all the pieces in place, including more personnel, financial backing, and the right location.

Some Key Thoughts

Before we finish we want to give you two more important or key thoughts that we think need to be stated clearly. First the difference between Guilt and Shame and Understanding Negative Emotions.

Guilt or Shame

It is important to understand and then consistently remind ourselves that guilt is different than shame. Shame and guilt are often spoken of as if they were interchangeable and have identical meanings. We believe that is not the case.

The two feelings have very different meanings and are usually generated by two different types of actions. Studies show that shame is a key to keeping someone in a destructive cycle of addiction and/or trauma. So the importance of understanding the difference between the two is highly important and then how shame works.

Look at the following charts to see what we mean:

Guilt	Shame
Guilt addresses only the behavior.	**Shame** is a devaluation of self.
Guilt draws you to God.	**Shame** pushes you away from God.
Guilt says "I did something bad."	**Shame** says "I am something bad."
Guilt is about a behavior.	**Shame** is about being.
Guilt is produced by the Holy Spirit, by my conscience letting me know I've said or done something wrong.	**Shame** is produced by Satan telling me that something is wrong with me as a human being, or as a person.
Guilt serves a purpose of being an internal conscience to help prevent us from acting out on harmful actions.	**Shame** is not feeling that we did a wrong thing; it is a feeling that we are the wrong thing.
Guilt feelings are generated by our beliefs about our actions.	**Shame** is a feeling that is generated by our wrong beliefs about ourselves as a person.

Shame Filter

EVENT

FEELINGS OF VULNERABLITY

SHAME FILTER

SELF – CONTEMPT
beats me up!

OTHER – CONTEMPT
beats you up!

ISOLATION

EMPTINESS

Cleaning Our Shame Filter:

1. Acknowledge shaming ways.
2. Derive value from God, not performance.
3. Be honest about: the event, your core feelings related to events.
4. Find yourself on the chart and work back up to event and vulnerable feelings.
5. Reach out to others for help.
6. Address obstacles: addictions, brain issues, toxic environment.

- Shame Filter developed by Mark MacDonald

Understanding Negative Emotions

Suzanne remembers going to *Walt Disney World* as a child. She doesn't remember much about that vacation at all, but she does remember going on the ride, "It's a Small World." So, when she returned to Disney as an adult and saw that ride her mind went back to those very special memories of her childhood family vacation.

Another pleasant memory was when Suzanne was in high school. She chose not to cheer one year for her soccer team. She regretted that choice since she was dating a guy on the team. She tried to go to all the games even though she wasn't cheering, but normally would not go to the away games. SMICS ended up going to the playoffs that year. Her dad took her to both the regional playoffs, as well as the national championship playoffs so that she could be there and not miss the excitement. SMICS did not win the Championship that year but came in second place. The hotel that they stayed in for the regional's was on the main interstate going south on I-65. To this day, as we pass that location, her mind floods with good memories of that event. The hotel is not even there any longer, but when she sees the exit her mind goes back to those good memories with her dad.

Our experiences of life through our families of origin, other significant relationships, as well as the experiences within our coupleship, have an ongoing impact in our lives. Current situations or actions create what we call **triggers** of things from the past, sometimes with great intensity both positively and negatively. We are sure you can think back in your mind to your favorite family vacation that you had as a child. Do you often have a smell, a taste, a song, or a sound that will trigger that memory? That would be a *positive trigger*.

We also can be *triggered negatively*. When that happens often we find ourselves trying to cope by seeking to *exit* the situation or relationship for a time, because it hurts so badly. When we identify a negative trigger you must *bring it out of the darkness and expose it to the light*. Doing that on a consistent basis is a healthy practice for each of us. We believe it is necessary for true recovery to occur to understand *Triggers* and *Exits* better.

A "trigger" is any kind of stimulus that reminds you of some earlier experience. As we already said, a trigger can be both positive and negative. But our purpose now is to focus on what to do when we are triggered negatively.

Negative triggers cause deep pain and are often magnified greatly. Here is a good example of a negative trigger. We were on a date about two years after Paul's trip to Amsterdam. We were actually having a wonderful evening, free of conflict, and we felt very close to each other. We were walking through the Galleria Mall in Birmingham and looking at all the kiosks in the middle of the mall. There was one that was selling paintings. We were walking around looking at the beautiful paintings, holding hands, and talking and then *WHAM*! Suzanne saw a painting of the canals of Amsterdam or Venice. Suzanne's hand slipped out of Paul's very abruptly. Her entire countenance changed because it reminded her of the trip that Paul took to Amsterdam that changed our world forever. This was a very magnified, hurtful, and negative **trigger**! We can be triggered negatively in many ways. Some examples include:

- A Place, Person, Picture, Event

- A Smell, Taste, Song

- A Look, Mannerism, Phrase

- A Name, Movie, TV show

- An Emotion (Loneliness, Hurt, Fear, Unmet Expectations)

What do you do with these triggers? How do you react to your negative triggers? So often we have learned ways to *cope* with them. Coping with triggers is a way to escape, numb, or avoid the pain, hurt, or the feeling of fear or anxiety that the trigger brings to us. Some examples include:

- Sleep, Television, Zone Out, Tune Out, Take a Bath

- Withhold Love, Get Sick, Silent Treatment, Withdraw

- Deflect, Try to Fix, Blame, Get Overly Dramatic

- Addictions (Porn, Masturbation, Alcohol, Food, Fantasy, Smoke, Shop)

- Raised Voice, Anger Outburst, Sulk, Destroy Things

- Take a Walk, Go Outside, Physically Leave, Exercise

Every one of us reacts to triggers differently. But we need to understand that there are times we do not even realize that we have been triggered. We wake up in a bad mood for no good reason. We don't understand why our child is getting on our last nerve, or we want to plow through that person driving too slowly down the highway. Where is all that negative emotion or anger coming from?

Finding out where the trigger is, often will come after you have *exited* without realizing it. We know that is true for us sometimes when one of us becomes angry. The person who is angry has *exited* without even realizing it. So, we have learned to stop and ask ourselves, "What has triggered me to the point where I want to shut down, express or even display anger?" *We believe that anger is a secondary emotion that is an expression of a deeper emotion.* When we can understand the deeper emotion we then can have control over shutting down or becoming angry. But each of us needs to first admit that we are triggered by something.

It is important to understand anger. To be able to understand where that negative emotion is coming from we have learn to take "*Time Outs*". We take them so that we will not take our negative emotions and express them in anger to each other. Most do not understand the source of the anger or that it is a "secondary emotion." Secondary, because it is not what is felt first, which is a "primary emotion." The primary emotion is what is felt immediately before we feel angry. <u>We always feel something else first before we get angry</u>. Many times we are unaware of the other emotion until it is looked at honestly. This is a good, basic understanding of anger. We have found that anger usually is a way to cover up or hide core emotions. We have categorized these core emotions into three categories - Past, Present, and Future.

Anger

Past	Present	Future
Hurt	Unfilled Expectation Frustration	Fear Anxiety

How is this seen in everyday life? It begins with you being in the present. We were walking down the mall holding hands with each other. Wham! Suzanne sees the painting of the canals. Trigger! Where did she go? She went to somewhere in the past. She felt the pain of the hurt that happened two years earlier. So, Suzanne dropped Paul's hand in response to that trigger. Did that have anything to do with what Paul was saying or doing at that moment? No, it was something that he did two years earlier. She had already forgiven him of that event though. So, why did that still trigger her? Because she is human and she can forgive, but that is not to say that she has forgotten the event, and it can become a very hurtful memory in present moments.

Now, for you who are reading this book and have just experienced a hurtful situation, we do not want you to loose heart. But we do want to be honest and normalize the moments when you will be triggered. Suzanne does not still have those triggers, at least to where they hurt so badly. Now she can look at pictures of the canals, see the beauty of the picture, and not get so hurt. Because God has healed that wound and yet, we do not forget the hurt that she felt so long ago. She can appreciate the fact that it changed her and has made her into a better person. God uses the wounds of our past to conform us into the likeness of Christ, if we let Him.

There are other moments, when we do not have the same kind of experience. We may not understand quite as clearly where the trigger has come from, as Suzanne did with the painting of the canals. It may be a particular look. For years, if Paul rubbed his head, Suzanne would go into a rage! It made her feel as if he was completely irritated with her. There was a message that she heard basically all her life that she was stupid. Where did that message come from?

Suzanne cannot pin point even one particular event in her life, but only knows that she has felt it from very early on in her life. Living with siblings, you cannot grow up untouched from negative emotions. Suzanne is sure that a lot of it came from her own perspective, but the reality is, the enemy (Satan) was whispering messages to her from a very early age. She truly believed that others thought she was stupid. She also believed early on that her voice did not matter. Suzanne believed that her only chance to be accepted in this world was to look pretty. So, if ever she felt the tone, the look, or the sound of anything close to the message that she was stupid, she was triggered to a feeling from a very early age.

It is interesting how we can become the age of our earliest painful memory. When we feel that we are seen as stupid, too much, or unacceptable it is a challenge for us to not revert into childlike behavior. We did not grasp the understanding of the "*inner child*" pain quite so much until we witnessed a grown man who actually appeared as though he was in his early teens sitting in our office. As we were talking, he was hearing messages that he was not worthy to be with. This was manifested in his fear of abandonment by his wife. To cope or avoid feeling abandoned, he actually abandoned her first. He worked long hours to avoid any intimacy with her, and he cheated on her multiple times. He was sure that he would be rejected by her and she would leave him.

When he heard that she felt he had behaved inappropriately, he heard, "You are a failure, you aren't worthy of my love, I deserve better than you." He became verbally aggressive in his speech and behaved as though he was a child, with the rolling of the eyes, glaring at her as if he wanted to kill her, and pouting. Later we discovered that his father had an affair and left his mother when he was twelve years old. So as he sat in our office, he was acting like that little boy did during those years of abandonment, even though he was the one abandoning presently.

Understanding triggers is to know that we hear or experience things in present situations which results in an *unmet expectation* or *frustration*. This then can send us either into the past where we feel *hurt* or into the future where we feel *fear* or *anxiety*. And often this can happen simultaneously. Gary J. Oliver says this:

> *"The people to whom we give the most time and energy, in whom we invest the greatest amount of love and other emotions, are the ones we have the highest expectations of and are the ones with the greatest potential to*

trigger painful emotions such as fear, hurt,
frustration, and eventually anger"

Mad About Us: Moving from Anger to
Intimacy with Your Spouse
By Gary J. Oliver, Carrie Oliver

We have found, and now teach to our couples, that if we are triggered, we have to understand what the primary emotions are and where they are coming from to be able to get back into our present *adult self*. We have learned to ask ourselves several questions to identify where the emotion of anger is coming from.

1. What/who hurt me?

2. What was my expectation that went unmet?

3. What was I frustrated about?

4. What was I afraid of?

5. What was I worried about?

If we stop and ask ourselves these questions we can control the emotion of anger. When we are experiencing the emotion of anger, we can avoid getting angry and even going to **emotionally flooding**. Even if we are being accused of being angry and we don't think that we are, we can become angry without even understanding what the anger is all about.

One of the things that we talk about the most with a couple is *emotional flooding,* especially in the beginning. We do this because we know a lot about this subject as a couple. As we have become more and more healthy in recovery, it is easier for us to keep from emotional flooding; but it wasn't always this way. As we said earlier, we learned that anger is a secondary emotion and is a way of coping with the primary emotions of either fears or hurts. Suzanne, who admits and openly talks about her struggle in this area, did in depth study on this subject. The following is what she has learned and teaches each of our couples:

Emotional Flooding
by Suzanne Talley

When I learned that my anger was a consequence from my insecurities due to fears or hurts I was able to stop the flooding. Something that I learned early on was that if I would give myself a timeout, I could calm down enough to identify the primary emotion that was fueling my anger and could turn into rage. The term **emotional flooding** refers to the adrenalin and cortisol stress hormones that flood your body causing a *fight* or *flight* response. Through *Dr. John Gottman's* research we have learned that if a couple would take a *time-out* before the emotional flooding, it will help to not say things that you regret later.

What happens in emotional flooding is the heart rate elevates up to ninety to a hundred beats per minute and will go into the red alert. This is what Dr. Gottman refers to as **D**iffuse **P**hysiological **A**rousal or *DPA*, which is a **Sympathetic Nervous System (SNS)** response designed by God to escape danger. So, <u>when we begin to emotionally flood our bodies naturally go into defense mode</u>. The adrenaline enters your blood stream and you are in a mode of *fight* or *flight*, which feels like intense fear, anxiety, or anger.

You cannot fight for intimacy in a defense mode conversation, so your best option is to stop the flooding, and you do that by walking away from the conversation by asking for a *timeout*. It has been proven that to take a minimum of twenty minutes (we recommend thirty minutes) allows those chemicals to pass throughout your nervous system and exit your body. If you do not take the minimal twenty minute timeout to begin the calming effect, your heart rate will remain elevated and you will continue to dump adrenaline into your system, thus clouding your ability to think clearly. So how do we do that?

Healthy Exiting

Often, when we begin to help people deal with flooding, they understand they need a minimal twenty minute timeout, but they have a "hit and run" way of exiting. They know they have to get away from the situation and calm down but they fail to be respectful to their spouse as they take the timeout. We have developed a safe way for couples to request a timeout without attacking the other spouse and before emotionally flooding.

When I first started to change, I took a timeout as soon as I began to feel my heart rate elevate. Since we do not walk around with heart monitors on, it would be difficult to know when our heart rate has elevated to the appropriate number of beats per second to be in a state of *DPA*. Therefore, to keep from going to the point of no return, as soon as you begin to feel signs of frustration, hurt, or anxiety, take a minimal twenty minute timeout by requesting from your spouse to *table the conversation*. I ask in this way; "I need a time out, can we please table this conversation?" This helps Paul to know that I am not avoiding the conversation but need time to evaluate what emotions I have underneath the emotion of anger. *Tabling* is not the same thing as stuffing emotions or avoiding them. It is me saying that I need time to cool down and have self-exploration to be able to express in a proper way what I am feeling.

Sometimes, I am just stubborn and refuse to table the argument, thus creating an unsafe place for me and my husband. He feels my anger and has two choices; he can get angry himself and flood, which doesn't help the situation at all, or he can choose to be the hero in this scenario and ask some helpful questions and statements.

- What is it that you are hearing me say?

- I can understand how that could trigger you.

- I am sorry that what I said triggered you.

- I need a timeout myself. Can we talk about this later today?

If the timeout is not respected by the non-flooding spouse, you need to understand that you are only going to make the flooding spouse flood worse by continuing to try and reason with them. They do not have the capability to think clearly because of what is happening inside of them, and they will become more aggressive. You MUST remove yourself or call for help if boundaries are not respected. NEVER allow anyone male or female to disrespect you or physically hurt you. If you do not learn to have self-respect, how can your spouse learn to respect you?

So, the key is to understand *triggers* and the use of *timeouts* (or *"tabling"*) before flooding happens so that you can be respectful to yourself first and then to your spouse. Taking the minimal twenty minutes to calm down and come back with a different perspective is the key to learning to have healthy conflict and healthy conversations. It has changed my life to learn and understand that my husband is not my enemy, but to understand that I am no different than the rest of the world, including my husband, in that we are all wounded individuals in need of a Savior.

We hope that has been as helpful as it has been for us.

Chapter FOURTEEN

The Key to True Intimacy: Confession

How to Tell the Truth

Paul can remember like it was yesterday, sitting in the basement waiting for Suzanne to arrive home. He had been up for over 30 hours with very little sleep and sitting all by himself. It was the loneliest, most fearful, and emptiest feeling he had ever experienced. After Paul told her what he had done and Suzanne got up from crying, she was very angry and began to ask Paul questions about the events that had taken place. Suzanne wanted details and Paul gave them to her. Those details hurt her deeply at the moment and continued to hurt her for many years to come.

At the time, we did not know the right thing to do, or the right thing to say, or not to say. Suzanne asked and Paul answered. We want to be clear when that event happened that was a *partial confession* and is not what we are writing about. Partial confessions take place at volatile times, in the heat of the moment, are not very healing, but usually very damaging to the relationship. In the therapeutic world this would be called a *Partial Disclosure* as apposed to a *Full Disclosure*. Disclosure by definition is *the act of something* and in this case confession. We have chosen to use the term confession (true confession is full and never partial) as this is what God has commanded us to do both to Him (I John 1:9) and to others (James 5:16).

We have found this scenario to be true for many of the couples that come to see us in our ministry today. They have had some kind of partial confession because a spouse was discovered in their sin, or they couldn't handle keeping a secret anymore, so they had to tell their spouse. Many spouses have their minds filled with unnecessary images and details that are not beneficial to the healing of their marriage but a hindrance.

The term confession is a very scary and intimidating time for both spouses and should be handled in the most healing way possible. Our purpose in writing this is to explain the importance of why we should engage in confession, how to find safe people to assist in Telling the Truth, and how to do it so that it will not be damaging but honest account on what has happened.

Why should I Tell the Truth?

We believe this is the first thing to address because some say it should never be done. They don't see the benefit of doing it. We think it should be done, but only in a proper way, which we will clearly lay out. Listen to our mentor as he explains the reason why it is important. We will use Eli's words because we do not think we could explain it any clearer. Eli explains it this way:

> "Integrity is telling myself the truth. And honesty is telling the truth to other people." Spencer Johnson, M.D.

> When it comes to informing your spouse of boundaries that have been violated, the whole truth is always the standard to follow. In a relationship where deception and lies have existed to cover an addiction (*or any sin* - added by us), trust has been violated. Rigorous honesty promptly revealed is vital in earning the essential component of trust in any relationship and maintaining integrity in that relationship.

> Withholding the truth because you think you'll hurt your spouse by disclosing it is flawed thinking. This illusion is often used by the addict (the offender) and sometimes encouraged by naïve counselors and some misled individuals in the recovery community.

> In reality, it's the behavior which is being covered up with the deception that hurts

your spouse, and although she or he feels pain when the truth is revealed, the truth was never what caused the pain. It was caused by the betraying action.

In actuality, using the excuse of wanting to protect your spouse from "being hurt" is an attempt to protect yourself and to manage your spouse's emotions or control their decisions.

> *"The Lord detests lying lips, but he delights in men who are truthful."*
> **Proverbs 12:22**

We base the need for confession on principles found throughout the Bible. The purpose of confession is twofold: *fellowship* and *healing*. The two passages that stand out to us in encouraging this process are I John 1 and James 5.

The first passage (I John 1) states that we are to *walk in the Light as God is light.* In this passage *walking in the light* is evident in two ways: Fellowship with others, in this case your spouse, and Cleansing of sin by Jesus. If we cannot have fellowship with God and *walk in darkness* it should be assumed that it cannot be done in our marriages either. Our marriage is the most intimate relationship outside of our relationship with God. Our relationship with God is even compared to a marriage relationship throughout the scriptures. By that we should see how important marriage is to God.

> I John 1:5-7 says, *"This is the message we have heard from Him and announce to you, that God is Light, and in Him there is no darkness at all. If we say that we have fellowship with Him and yet walk in the darkness, we lie and do not practice the truth; but **if we walk in the Light** as He Himself is in the Light, **we have fellowship with one another** and **the blood of Jesus His Son cleanses us from all sin**."*

True fellowship does not and cannot be experienced based on deceit, lies and/or hidden things! To have a true fellowship or intimate relationship it must be based on the foundation of truth.

The second passage is found in James 5:16, *"Therefore, **confess your sins to one another**, and pray for one another **so that you may be healed**. The effective prayer of a righteous man can accomplish much."*

True healing for an individual or couple will not come without confession or telling the truth. When things are kept in the darkness it controls in many ways but most powerfully by shame. Paul's shame controlled him and it continually drove him back to his addictions. Ephesians 5:11 says, *"Do not participate in the unfruitful deeds of darkness, but instead even expose them."*

Paul was stricken by the shame of his sin because he kept his sin in the darkness, but once it was exposed to the light he found freedom. Once a true confession had been made, first to the group of men at the first workshop he attended, he felt a freedom he had never felt before. At that workshop, we were given a homework assignment to aid us in the telling of our stories. Upon returning home, we were able to use this homework to tell the truth fully in a non-damaging way. It was profoundly healing for us individually as well as in our marriage. It is our opinion that it should not be done alone, as a couple, but with the help of safe people, and we will help you identify safe people later.

The result of Paul's *full* confession was the reviving of his soul, but also a revival in the other men at that workshop. Over the weeks, months, and years after that workshop we have seen revival around us continue, which ultimately brought us back to full-time ministry. There are several Biblical examples (Matthew 3:6 and Acts 19:18) that show us through confession of sin revival breaks out.

How do you find "Safe People" to assist in a Confession?

Galatians 6 explains for us who safe people are. Finding safe people is a scary thing in the church and it should not be that way. If the church would follow the instructions found here, it would be a safe oasis to those struggling in sin, as it should be. This is what it says:

> *"Brethren, even if anyone is caught in any trespass, you* **who are spiritual***, restore such a one in a spirit of gentleness; each one looking to yourself, so that you too will not be tempted. Bear one another's burdens, and thereby fulfill the law of Christ. For if anyone thinks he is something when he is nothing, he deceives himself. But each one must examine his own work,"* Galatians 6:1-4

The Biblical mandate to the restoration process is that it should be done by those *"who are spiritual"* and in doing so they will *"fulfill the law of Christ"*. After making that statement, the passage goes on to describe the characteristics of those who are spiritual. These spiritual people are the ones we classify as *safe people*.

These are not necessarily the leadership in a church, which is sad, because they should be the safest people that we could find. We have found that some churches are full of *Pharisaical leaders*. They judge, condemn, and don't restore. That grieves the heart of God. On the other hand, we have found many pastors and church leaders that are gentle and understanding, which is very refreshing and pleases the heart of God. So let us look at the characteristics found in Galatians 6, so that you can find safe people for your confession:

1. One that will not look down on you but *RESTORE* you.

"restore such a one"

2. One that will not condemn you but be *GENTLE* with you.

"spirit of gentleness"

3. One that will not judge you but *UNDERSTANDS* you.

4.

"one looking to yourself"

"For if anyone thinks he is something when he is nothing, he deceives himself"

4. One that will not talk about you but be *BURDENED* for you.

"bear one another's burdens"

We find here that safe people are described as the ones that have a heart to restore, be gentle, understanding (because they themselves struggle with sin), and someone who will walk with you helping you carry your burden.

What should the confession contain?

To explain what a confession should contain, we will start with what it should not contain. Confession is never associated with the word "partial" or half-truths. We have found in our own experience and in helping others recover from a betrayal that partial confession can be more damaging to the marriage than not doing anything at all. Partial confession allows the deception and lies to continue to exist. Sin continues to be covered up and trust will continue to be violated. Partial truth, or "partial" honesty, will destroy any earned trust that the relationship had built when more truth is discovered or confessed. As a result, any repair that the relationship has had is completely lost and it will make it even harder to regain.

Confession is not damaging if done properly. Partial confession is what is truly damaging because true intimacy, integrity, and fellowship in a relationship without the full truth are impossible. Without full truth there is a wall, a barrier, or a distance because you are not allowing yourself to be fully known by the other. We have heard it so many times, "why do I need to bring this all up again? We have dealt with it." Have you really? Having something "dealt with" can only be accomplished if it was fully dealt with honestly.

Our kids have always had the responsibility of doing the kitchen, on a rotating basis. When they would leave the kitchen we would often ask, "Was the kitchen done" and they would say "yes". By them saying yes we would assume it was all done. So if one of us would walk into the kitchen and see the counter tops not washed off, a pan soaking in the sink, or the floor sticky we would be very disappointed. Why? Because we were told the kitchen was done, it was done in their minds, but in our reality it was not. Our point is partially dealing with it is not dealing with it at all in the mind of the betrayed spouse.

Eli addressed partial truth earlier when he said *"withholding the truth because you think you'll hurt your spouse by disclosing it is flawed thinking...In reality, it's the behavior which is being covered up with the deception that hurts your spouse, and although she or he feels pain when the truth is revealed, the truth was never what caused the pain. It was caused by the betraying action. In actuality, using the excuse of wanting to protect your spouse from "being hurt" is an attempt to protect yourself and to manage your spouse's emotions or control their decisions."*

What Eli is saying is what we have seen so many times in our ministry. The betrayer does not think their spouse can handle the truth. It seems to always come down to two self-deceptions.

The first self-deception is the betrayer thinks that they are strong and their spouse is weak. That is totally offensive to the one that has been betrayed. In reality the betrayer is the weaker one, evident by the fact that they are unable to control their own actions. They are the one who fell into sin, not their spouse.

The second self-deception is the betrayer claiming they are protecting their spouse. Reality is that they are protecting themselves. The betrayer usually fears that their spouse might leave them because of the full truth. Paul knows he did! If they do not fear them leaving they are at least fearing the reaction from their spouse once they receive the full truth, as Paul did.

So what is a *full* confession? It is complete honesty. We have found that it takes time and coaching of the betraying spouse to know what to say and what not to say. This is not to be interpreted that deception is taught, but that some details of the act of betrayal are not needed for true confession to happen. For an example, if the betrayal was with another person many times there is no need to give the details of what sexual acts were done, how they were done, and even sometimes where they were done. ***Those types of details destroy not restore.***

When a confession is done, if too many details are given, the betrayed spouse will have unnecessary "triggers" that they will have to deal with for a long time, maybe a life time. This is why it is so important to get help on how to give your confession before the betrayer tells their spouse. All those details must be worked through beforehand to insure their confession is full, complete, and completely honest.

Once confession is done, questions for clarification can be asked. Those who are there as a guide or support should be careful to make sure that questions are not leading for the betrayer to give unnecessary details to the one betrayed. This is a hard, delicate stage to navigate so it is always good to have safe people who have had some experience in doing this. If you cannot find any experienced safe people in your church, which will sometimes be hard to do, we recommend that you involve an experienced counselor that understands and agrees with the purpose of confession (Full Disclosure).

We have also seen that coaching of the betrayed spouse is necessary as well. They must understand what the purpose of the confession is and what it is not. They must understand that unnecessary details can cripple their recovery from this betrayal or at least really slow it down. If there is a solid trust with the person(s) coaching them, then they can encourage the betrayed to use this time "to come clean" as well. This is almost impossible sometimes, but when it is possible it becomes a beautiful time of healing for the couple.

In our ministry we take confession very seriously and take a lot of time to prepare for it. Most of the time, but not all, we allow both spouses to tell their stories to each other at the same time. As a result, understanding and empathy can be given and received at the same time. It slows down the process but it allows it to be truly healing. There are cases because the sin has been completely hidden, that a *full* confession of just one spouse is given. In those times, even more time is given to prepare because of the seriousness of the sin, and that is a discussion for the future

Conclusion of PART THREE

We pray as you read Part Three that you will see the hand of God on us and on this ministry. We love telling our story so that people can see how God is always faithful and that He does *work all things out for our good.*

We hope that you have gained some knowledge of how to improve your marriage, and see the importance of being involved in an *intentionally intrusive, Christ-centered, grace driven, redemptive community* (Paul Tripp). Our desire is to help churches all over the United States and around the world to do this very thing. The church needs to be a functioning community, not just a place to gather to worship and go home. Many churches have Sunday School and/or small groups that in principle do that, but often it becomes just another activity of the church and not an active community.

We hope we have helped you evaluate what kind of community you have, and if change needs to happen that you will be a key component to that change. If you are not involved in a community get involved in one. If you would like our help in setting up, organizing, and facilitating this type of community please feel free to contact us.

Conclusion of Restored

We have found that most members, pastors, and church leaders feel all alone in their everyday lives and we hope that this book has been a wakeup call. We are all in need of recovery from our core beliefs that are really simply unbelief.

Many statistical studies find the divorce rate is higher in the church then it is in the world. Read what Albert Mohler Jr. has said:

> ...*evangelical Protestants divorce, higher than almost any other religious group and above the national average ... this creates a significant credibility crisis when evangelicals then rise to speak in defense of marriage.*
>
> *The sanctity of human life is a cause that demands our priority ....legalized same-sex marriage demands our attention....but divorce harms many more lives.... Children are left without fathers, wives without husbands, and homes are forever broken. Fathers are separated from their children, and marriage is irreparably undermined as divorce becomes routine and accepted.*
>
> "Divorce -- The Scandal of the Evangelical Conscience,"
> by R. Albert Mohler, Jr., President-Southern Baptist Theological Seminary

This is what others are saying:

> *"We cannot very well argue for the sanctity of marriage as a crucial social institution while we blithely go about divorcing...at a rate that destabilizes marriage,*
> *— Mark Galli, senior managing editor of Christianity Today*

> *According to a <u>Barna Research Group</u> report, fundamentalist Christians have the highest divorce rate, followed by Jews and Baptists...*

We say that the church is in a crisis and we feel that we need to be part of the solution and not part of the problem. We must speak out and try to wake up the church, as it seems to put a blind eye to the problem of divorce.

My Family Lab in answering the question "Is <u>Serial Monogamy</u> a modern version of polygamy?" found the following...

> *When divorce and remarriage rates are high, as in the United States, people engage in <u>Serial Monogamy</u>. That is, they marry several people, but one at a time — they marry, divorce, remarry, redivorce, and so on.*

We cannot ignore the facts by the *National Fatherhood Initiative*:

In America, 24.35 million children (33.5 percent) live absent their biological father.

And in the state of Alabama the facts are:

According to Alabama DHR and the U.S. Department of Health and Human Services statistics: Children with limited or no contact with one of their biological parents accounts for:

- *63% of youth suicides*
- *75% of juvenile drug abuse*
- *85% of youths in prison*
- *71% of school dropouts*
- *71% of teen pregnancies*
- *90% of homeless and runaway children*

We must wake up and stop the cycle of divorce. The ministry of CMIC is called to that mission. If you would like for us to speak to your organization, at your church, or lead a Workshop just let us know. Please get involved and let us know how we can help by contacting us through our web page:

www.christianmarriagesincrisis.com

Made in the USA
Columbia, SC
19 January 2020